Growing
Up
to
God

Eight Steps in Religious Development

Growing
Up
to
God

Eight Steps in Religious Development

John J. Gleason, Jr.

ABINGDON
Nashville

GROWING UP TO GOD: EIGHT STEPS IN RELIGIOUS DEVELOPMENT

Copyright © 1975 by Abingdon Press

Library of Congress Cataloging in Publication Data

GLEASON, JOHN J. 1934-
  Growing up to God; eight steps in religious development.
  Includes bibliographical references.
  1. Psychology, Religious. 2. Erikson, Erik Homburger, 1902-
I. Title.
BL53.G58   200'.19   74-17093

ISBN 0-687-15972-5

Scripture quotations are from *The Jerusalem Bible*, copyright
© 1966 by Darton, Longman & Todd, Ltd. and Doubleday &
Company, Inc. Used by permission of the publisher.

A portion of Chapter 7 appeared in the Spring 1971 issue of *Voices*.

MANUFACTURED BY THE PARTHENON PRESS AT
NASHVILLE, TENNESSEE, UNITED STATES OF AMERICA

Dedicated to the Memory of My First Father-God

Contents

Preface

Chapter

1. The Immediate Context for a Developmental
   Psychology of Religion 13

2. A Developmental Psychology of
   Religion Delineated 21

3. Basic Trust and the Doctrine of God 26

4. Autonomy and Good and Evil 38

5. Initiative and Sin—Redemption 49

6. Industry and Works 62

7. Identity and Man 74

8. Intimacy and Christology 89

9. Generativity and Creation 105

10. Integrity and Eschatology 117

11. Conclusion 130
    Notes 133

Preface

As I sat down in a large ballroom at the Newton, Massachusetts, Marriott Motor Hotel during the 1970 Joint Fall Conference of the Association for Clinical Pastoral Education, Inc., and the American Association of Pastoral Counselors, I felt smugly satisfied. I had just met the challenge of facing an ACPE Certification and Accreditation Committee and convincing them of my readiness for certification as a full supervisor.

Then Orlo Strunk, Jr., began his address, "Relationships of Psychology of Religion and Clinical Pastoral Education." Before he was through, I had heard a new and equally demanding challenge.

Just as clinical pastoral education provides raw data for the psychologist of religion and consciously reminds him of these data, so too must the psychologist of religion confront the clinician with the necessity of sharing his insights in styles acceptable to others besides himself and his fellow clinicians. And the clinically oriented must learn to do this in terms of the other's criteria as well as his own. If this does not take place, a great deal of clinical "knowledge" becomes private or at least fraternalistically secret, driving deep wedges between endeavors which ought to be in creative dialogue.

9

Further, Bernard Spilka, writing in the Spring, 1970, Review of Religious Research, envisions current shifts from behavioristic, adjustmental, and mental health models of the nature of man to humanistic and actionistic formulations as an opportunity for a rapprochement of theological and psychological principles. He proposes their integration in a "Theological-Psychology of Religion," an empirically based religious psychology with solid footing in objective research, yet not detached from explicit theological values.

A developmental psychology of religion as elaborated in this study seeks to move toward Spilka's dreamed of "Theological-Psychology of Religion" and to respond in part to Strunk's challenge.

John J. Gleason, Jr.
Spring, 1973

Growing
Up
to
God

Eight Steps in Religious Development

1

The Immediate Context for a
Developmental Psychology of Religion

A. The Life of Erik Erikson

The immediate context for a developmental psychology of religion can be summed up in two words—Erik Erikson.[1] Erikson was born in Frankfurt, Germany, on June 15, 1902. His parents were natives of Denmark. Before Erik was born his father and mother separated, and she went to Germany to be with friends. Mrs. Erikson fell in love with Erik's pediatrician, and when Erik was three she married Dr. Homburger. Erik was known as Erik Homburger for several years and for some time had no knowledge of his genetic sire. When he found out that Dr. Homburger was not his physical father, his great fascination with and interest in identity problems seemed to be triggered. He is almost preoccupied with and most of his works sooner or later end up involved in questions of identity and its development.

Erikson went to primary school from the age of six to the age of ten, then to high school until he was eighteen. He then spent a year traveling around Germany, walking through the Black Forest, enjoying a sort of "lone wolf" experience. He enrolled in an art school, but soon quit and went to Munich, enrolling in a second art school briefly. His work there has been described as very individual. He did large woodcuts that took physical strength as well as artistic ability. After two years he moved to Florence where he began association with a group of young writers and artists, the most significant of whom was a man named Peter Blos, now an American child psychoanalyst, but at that time an aspiring writer.

At the age of twenty-five Erik went back to the area where he had originally been enrolled in art school. He got a letter from Peter Blos inviting him to come to Vienna. There Blos had been engaged in the conduct of a freewheeling, progressive school for American children. Erikson was to tutor the children of a wealthy New York lady who was undergoing psychoanalysis with Sigmund Freud. After some correspondence back and forth, Erikson decided that he would go to Vienna. There he had free rein to set up and operate an expanded version of this school for English-speaking children whose parents, and even some of the children themselves, were undergoing analysis with Freud or Freud's daughter, Anna.

Almost naturally, then, Erikson got into analysis himself and became a patient of Anna Freud's. He would go for his analytic hour in the morning and then teach for the rest of the day. This was in a much less formal way than analysis is done now. He socialized with the whole family. At one point in 1930 when Sigmund Freud was fighting old age and gradually spreading cancer of the mouth, Freud invited Erikson to Berlin with the family while he was undergoing medical treatment. Erikson continued his analysis with Anna in Berlin.

Having enrolled in the Psychoanalytic Institute in Vienna, Erikson had by 1933 become settled at last in his vocational identity—that of child psychoanalyst. When the time came for the Analytic Institute members to decide on his status, instead of granting him the usual associate status they granted him full status which not only was a tribute to his talent, but also an act enabling him to make plans to leave Vienna. By then the Nazi clouds were gathering, and Hitler was rapidly moving to power. In the meantime, Erikson had met a dazzling young woman, Joan, with whom he fell in love. By 1933 they were married and two of their children had come along. Emigrating to the United States with his family, Erikson set up shop in Boston as the city's only child psychoanalyst.

B. The Work of Erik Erikson

Shortly after his arrival in Boston, he enrolled in Harvard as a Ph.D. candidate in clinical psychology, but he still found academia stifling and dropped out of the program. But, by then, some of the papers that he had written and some of the work that he was doing, not only with the children of the well-to-do but in a clinic in a Boston ghetto, had begun to build his reputation. He is now recognized as an outstanding contributor to ego psychology. He has written several impressive works, among which is *Childhood and Society*. He sets forth in chapter 7 the essence of his developmental scheme.[2]

Young Man Luther deals with the struggles and identity crisis of the adolescent and young adult Luther. A recent effort, *Gandhi's Truth*, is a study of the middle age and creative time in the life of the great Mahatma Gandhi. He has also written *Insight and Responsibility*, *Identity: Youth and Crisis*, and many monographs and articles for journals.[3]

His greatest contribution is the way he built on Freud's framework. Freud found and believed that sexuality does not begin with adolescence. It is a part of humanity from the outset. And by sexuality Freud meant more than specific maleness or femaleness, mere genitality. Rather he defined it very broadly to include the capacity of human beings for all kinds of pleasure. He felt from his study of people and from his own analysis that there are distinct stages in the development of this sexuality. The first stage is the oral stage in which the focus is on pleasures involving the mouth. This is most evident and lively in the first year of life when all the attention and pleasure, or lack of it, focus on the baby being fed and expressing itself orally by crying, sucking, and, as the teeth begin to come in, biting.

The second stage is the anal stage, according to Freud, in which toilet training becomes an important part of the child's life in part because it symbolizes the battle for control of his own life as well as the battle for control of his sphincters, his muscle control. Here the attention is on the other end of the digestive tract, the anal orifice.

Freud's most startling hypothesizing concerned what happens to people in ages three to five or six. In what he called the phallic stage, the Oedipal complex is dramatized in the life of the child. Every male child desires to take his mother away from the father; every female child desires to take her father from the mother. The child wants the parent of the opposite sex with all the murderous impulses that this stirs up and all the accompanying guilt. In a satisfactory resolution of the struggle the child discovers that he cannot compete with the parent of the same sex, so he does the next best thing. He or she identifies with the parent of the same sex. The little boy tries to be like Daddy, or the little girl tries to be like Mommie. If you can't wipe them out, you model yourself after them. This part of his theory shocked society, especially the religious community.

Erikson came along and built upon Freudian theory which had focused primarily upon childhood, early childhood at that. Freud did have something to say about what he called the latency period that followed the Oedipal years and then about mature genitality. But Erikson's great contribution is that he hypothesized an eight-stage series of life crises that includes what happens to people from birth to death. He says in the same way that botany has discovered that in the development of plant life there comes a fullness of time, an epigenetic moment in which a certain something is supposed to happen, that is, there is a certain moment in which seeds begin to sprout and another moment in which buds begin to form, leaves begin to open, and the flower begins to develop, so, in the same way developmentally certain things are to happen at certain critical times in the life cycle of human beings within the sphere of emotions.

17

C. The Theoretical Framework for a Developmental Psychology of Religion

The first crisis that Erikson hypothesizes is directly compatible with, although not the same as, Freud's oral stage. Erikson, heeding anthropological, cultural, sociological, as well as psychosexual considerations, says that in the first year of life all of us have a crisis in which we learn or fail to learn what he calls basic trust. In his scheme of things, it is basic trust versus mistrust. In the first year of life, in this first psychosocial crisis, the significant person is the mother or the mother figure. The psychosocial modality involved is to get and give in return, to take in.

The second psychosocial crisis that Erikson hypothesizes is one roughly equivalent to Freud's second stage, the anal stage, in which Erikson says that we learn as two-, three-, and four-year-olds the sense of autonomy, or we fail to learn it and are thereby left with extensive feelings of shame and doubt. The significant people involved in this are the parental persons, both parents. The psychosocial modalities that are involved here are to hold or to let go—literally when is it acceptable to relieve the bowels and bladder, and when is it not? Then symbolically, who is in charge of me —myself or my parents?

Then his third psychosocial crisis is what he calls initiative versus guilt. This stage again is roughly equated with Freud's Oedipal stage during the fourth, fifth, and sixth years of life. Within the basic family, Erikson believes that a person either develops his sense of initiative and, using the psychosocial modality literally to make, going after the parent of the opposite sex and also to make like, that is, playing, the person enhances and develops his senses of initiative and aggressiveness, or he ends up feeling extremely guilty. Initiative versus guilt.

The fourth developmental crisis, industry versus inferiority, is Erikson's refinement of Freud's latency stage in which Erikson recognizes as central the child's struggle for mastery of technological elements in (at least for Western society) the elementary school grades during the years between six or so and the onset of puberty. The psychosocial modalities at work here are to make things (to complete) and to make things together in school and neighborhood.

Crisis number five, according to Erikson, begins with puberty and lasts through adolescence. Here identity is the issue. Who am I? What does it mean to be a human being? A male or female human being? The danger is identity diffusion or role confusion, and the psychosocial modality is to be oneself (or not to be). The peer group takes on great significance in this stage.

Young adulthood brings on the life crisis Erikson distinguishes as intimacy versus isolation in which arrival at full physical genitality and power hopefully enables individuals to find partners in friendship, sex, competition, and cooperation. To lose and find oneself in another becomes the pertinent modality.

Now pressing on beyond the work of Freud into new territory, Erikson theorizes that the major concern of middle adulthood is whether or not one contributes significantly, whether or not generativity is achieved. Middle adults either produce in some measure children, ideas, and/or leadership, or slip, according to Erikson, into a condition he variously describes as stagnation and self-absorption. The modalities of middle adulthood are to make be and to take care of.

Finally, one ideally comes to a sense of integrity through the modalities of being through having been and facing not being. The question "Has life, my life in particular, been worth living?" is quietly answered in the affirmative with a sense of peace, meaning, maturity, and wisdom, or in the negative with bitter despair.[4]

2

A Developmental Psychology of Religion Delineated

A. The Basic Hypotheses

Even as Erikson built on Freud, so I am placing a religious overlay upon Erikson's eight ages. I am hypothesizing that religiously there comes a developmental epigenetic fullness of time wherein a particular theological lesson is learned at the level of the unconscious, at the feeling level; that particular theological doctrines are in focus at particular stages of human development; that the way the lesson is learned or distorted profoundly affects future religious lessons and development; that the subjective, gut-level experiencing of these lessons has more weight, more significance than later, more superficial, objective, cognitive, conscious lessons.[1] To wit, in a conflict between one's gut-level experiencing of one's first god—one's mother—as rejecting and harsh on the one hand and one's conscious-level learning of the attributes of God in catechism class or Sunday school on the other hand, one responds primarily out of one's early, feeling-level lesson about the nature of one's first god; that it becomes a lifelong task, the essential personal religious task, to sort out and distinguish between the nature of one's first god or gods and the nature of God.

B. Some Assumptions

Once, in a slightly (but not totally) tongue-in-cheek essay, I ventilated some of my anger at scientists who have, on the grounds of so-called scientific objectivity, disregarded attempts by religious and other investigators to study religious phenomena.[2] Lest I find myself guilty of my own charges, namely, that all orderly investigation has little meaning apart from an effort to acknowledge values, to elaborate some of the ways values enter into the investigative endeavor, and to state as explicitly as possible concretized value premises, I identify the following assumptions underlying this study.

1. Religion, operationally defined, can be meaningfully studied using methods appropriate to the defined subject matter.

2. The statistical methodology of experimental psychology is not appropriate to the defined subject matter.

3. The philosophy of investigation known as theoretical or logical positivism, in which only that which can be experimentally verified by physical laws is accepted as real, is rejected.

4. The philosophy of investigation referred to as the phenomenological approach, in which the re-

searcher tries to suspend many of his assumptions and asks for his subjects' own explanations of things he observes, is affirmed.

5. The ideographic or case study method is deemed appropriate, and is, therefore, chosen to illuminate the developmental hypotheses.

6. The study is, in its essence, more psychologically than theologically based in that it is focused at the level of observable phenomena and avoids attempts to move to the noumenal to prove, disprove, or even address the question of the existence and nature of God.

C. Some Definitions

Psychology is understood to be the scientific study of mental functioning, the systematic description and critical analysis of human behavior, the science of human behavior and experience. Since 1912 when James H. Leuba published *A Psychological Study of Religion* with forty-eight definitions of religion categorized under feeling, conduct, or belief, religion has been seen variously as instinct (Jastrow, Otto), derived reality (Starbuck), illusion (Freud, Marx), reverence for life (Schweitzer), encounter with the infinite (Murray), encounter with the finite (Hocking), ultimate concern (Johnson), the answer to want versus ought (Southard), a feeling of absolute dependence (Schleiermacher), a sense of unity (Spranger), an attitude (Thouless), a propitiation of superior powers (Frazer), belief (Martineau, James), a state of mind

(McTaggart), an aspect of culture (Kishimoto), and a way of solving personal or social problems (Pruyser), to name a few.[3]

For me religion is distinguishable at two levels—the societal and the individual. For society at large, religion comprises the bodies of knowledge, belief systems, behaviors, experiences, and institutions primarily concerned with ultimate values and ultimate solutions to problems of the meaning of life, and often includes concepts of deity, holiness, sin, redemption, and the like. For an individual person religion has to do both with the way he or she relates to and identifies with societal expressions, and furthermore, essentially with whatever he or she personally experiences as ultimately holy, sacred, and valuable, be it God, parent, spouse, offspring, vocation, acceptance, flag, possessions, happiness, holiness, or whatever.

Thus a person could be at one and the same time both irreligious in relation to societal expressions and profoundly religious in pursuit of clear, individual values and goals. Conversely, one could be both religious in terms of strong identification with and participation in one of society's institutional expressions of religion and personally irreligious by virtue of diffuse values and/or motivations.

Psychology of religion becomes "a systematic inquiry into those modes of being and projects of existence which meaningfully link this life to that which is believed to be supremely worthful,"[4] "the study of how the soul of man, both consciously and unconsciously, responds to the mystery of life and death, and to the impingement of an environment which in many ways

24

appears to be even more mysteriously alive than man himself."[5]

The aim of psychology of religion in general and of this developmental psychology of religion in particular, then, is to attempt to describe and interpret the personal meaning of religion and its social expression in light of classical norms for religion, wedding psychological developmental stages with theological doctrines in developmental focus.[6]

3

Basic Trust and the Doctrine of God

A. The Specific Hypothesis Elaborated

During the first year or so of life it is the mother or mother figure(s) who responds, in greater or lesser degree, to the expressed needs of the child—for milk, other nourishment, and the associated oral pleasures; for warmth, dryness, and general body comforts; for love; for laughter; for a general feeling of worth, satisfaction, well-being. Erikson's now familiar contention is that it is in this first year of life that the child experiences a developmental crisis in which he or she either learns basic trust or to varying degrees fails to learn basic trust (i.e., learns mistrust). I further postulate that at roughly this same developmental moment the mother or mother substitute is in a phenomenological, practical sense the child's first god, a god with a small g, and that, therefore, it is at this time that every child learns his or her first unconscious, feeling-level lesson about the nature and attributes of as yet undifferentiated gods, god, God.

When baby gets hungry, it cries. Mother-god is all-powerful (omnipotent) in the sense that she has it easily within her grasp to provide nourishment by offering her breast, preparing a bottle, or whatever. By the same token, she may use her power to withold the source of food for a little while or a long time, depending upon her assessment of appropriate feeding times, her general mood, and so on. Through the preponderance of pleasurable or discomfiting experiences of Mother-god's uses of power, the child is learning a feeling-level lesson: Mother-god uses her power to make me feel happy, or Mother-god uses her power to make me feel angry, uncomfortable, and unhappy.

Mother-god is all-knowing (omniscient) in the sense that she is sensitive to the differences between the cry that means "I am hungry," the cry that says, "I need changing," and the cry that expresses, "I am lonely and want to play." Yet for reasons of her humanity, abilities, and mood she may in fact at times be insensitive to the distinction between cries and their accompanying need. Again, the accumulation of mostly happy or unhappy experiences of Mother-god's knowing form the feeling conclusion: Mother-god uses her knowledge to make my life more pleasant or more miserable.

So, on down through the list of classical attributes of God one could pass, clearly identifying in the countless reenactments of the drama of mother nurturing child, the unconscious, foundational lessons being learned. God is love (or hate). God is merciful (or cruel). God is mighty (or weak). God is greatly to be feared (or appreciated). God is distant (or ever present). God is forgiving (or harsh). God is faithful (or faithless). God is to be trusted (or mistrusted). Or, probably most often, God is somewhere in between these extremes. Yet, as just stated, God remains intermingled with and indistinguishable from god or gods because of the inability of a child in his or her first year to engage in sophisticated abstract thought.

B. Religio-Cultural Referents

God as father is imagery commonly understood and accepted as long ago as in the days of ancient Greece. In polytheistic mythology (Homer's "Father Zeus") and in philosophical thought (Plato's "Maker and Father of this universe") the foundation was laid. For generations the Jews maintained that by God's choice of them to be his people, he had become their Father. At least one scholar holds that Jesus brought God as father to new heights by even sparing use of designations other than father in his life and in his choice of words.[1] A hurried survey of the listings under "father" in any Bible concordance will bear out the extensive usage of the term "father" by Jesus in describing God; there is at least one God/Father reference as far back as Psalms (89:26).[2]

God as mother finds its genesis and expression in animistic and Eastern religions; Mother Earth, or Earth Mother, as a principle, is in sharp contrast to Western Father God. Whereas, the traditionally Western Old Testament Father God has accumulated a preponderance of masculine attributes (holiness, jealousy, wrath, righteousness), Eastern Mother God manifests feminine qualities (acceptance, warmth, inclusiveness).[3] In a sense Jesus' strong emphasis on the fatherhood of God brought about a certain integration of feminine attributes with those masculine traits of the Old Testament God (grace, mercy, loving kindness).

God as mothering parent does find at least two interesting expressions in the Bible—in the garden of Eden account and in Psalm 91.

In Genesis 2:15–17 we read:

> Yahweh God took the man and settled him in the garden of Eden to cultivate and take care of it. Then Yahweh God gave the man this admonition, "You may eat indeed of all the trees in the garden. Nevertheless of the tree of the knowledge of good and evil you are not to eat, for on the day you eat of it you shall most surely die."

The parent-god nurtures his (her) creature in a safe, secure spot, meeting his every physical need (a bit later even providing him with a helpmate), yet, as good parents do, setting limits upon what is appropriate and what is inappropriate behavior.

Again in Psalm 91 God provides protection for his children from various dangers. Interestingly, the word trust is used specifically in verse two.

> If you live in the shelter of Elyon
> and make your home in the shadow of Shaddai,
> you can say to Yahweh, "My refuge, my fortress,
> my God in whom I trust!"
> He rescues you from the snares
> of fowlers hoping to destroy you;
> he covers you with his feathers,
> and you find shelter underneath his wings.

Here we find the startling imagery of the Old Testament God as Mother Hen!

With development of the church the masculine-feminine imagery polarized: God as father; church as mother and Mary as the mother of God. Mother church provided literally sanctuary for her children. Religious literature commonly uses feminine pronouns in conjunction with "church."

A tie-in of God and trust occurs at an unexpected cultural, even governmental, level in a nation usually extremely careful to separate matters of church from matters of state. United States coins and currency bear the motto In God We Trust.

C. Research Referents

Various researchers have attempted to examine the developmental aspects of understandings of God with special attention to gender and parental images.

Nelson and Jones sought to test Freud's hypothesis that God is in truth merely a grand projection of the father as he once appeared to the small child. Using a Q-sort procedure in which they obtained and compared descriptive patterns of God, Jesus, mother, and father, Nelson and Jones concluded that the image of God held by their subjects was more similar to the mother concept than to that of the father and that therefore the mother was probably most influential in the formation of the God concept.[4]

In a replication study Strunk got opposite results, finding the father concept more similar to the God concept among a small homogeneous sample of religiously trained Protestant students.[5]

Yet a third option has been offered that "a person's concept of God (i. e., a personal God) depends empirically on his experience of himself—as a self-directing person." Spilka speaks to the psychometric difficulties involved in the effort to correlate human referents with the God concept and then isolates eleven different God factors.[6]

Vergote *et al.*, investigating the relationship between maternal and paternal images of parents and God, had subjects rate their parents and God on eighteen maternal and eighteen paternal characteristics. Though in all samples the image of God is more paternal than maternal, in the American samples God appears to become gradually more maternal. American females and males both emphasize the paternal qualities of God (the males somewhat more so), unlike the French-speaking Belgian sample who emphasize the paternal qualities corresponding to their own sex.[7]

Assuming that children's verbal expressions do not give satisfactory information about the deeper religious life, Harms asked several thousand preschoolers, preadolescents, and postadolescents to draw a picture of God. The preschoolers' drawings he categorized as the fairy tale stage, wherein the images were of God as a king, often with a long, white beard, living in a golden house or in the clouds. The preadolescents fit into a realistic stage with the extensive appearance of symbols (crucifix, Jewish star) and human figures helping and influencing human life. The postadolescents he characterized in the individualistic stage with three distinct subgroupings. Group A, the conventional, portrayed the crucifix, the Madonna, gates of heaven, and so forth. Group B, more original, drew sunrises, humanitarian symbols, a flower budding winglike toward the sky. Group C, still more creative, contained Egyptian, Persian, Chinese, even Celtic symbols.[8]

In a more recent study I asked emotionally disturbed and "normal" adolescents to draw a picture of God. I isolated three categories listed from least mature to most mature—anthropomorphic, anthropomorphic-symbolic, symbolic.[9]

Contained in a massive text by British psychiatrist Frank Lake is extensive case material on the reliving of experiences of infancy, birth, and even prenatal sensations by psychiatric patients under the influence of LSD.[10]

In notes scrawled during one LSD session, a forty-seven-year-old clergyman said at one point, "It is as if I am struggling to be one person, saying one united 'yes' to one great breast-maternal Figure." Later, in an Easter morning reflection he wrote:

> I was re-experiencing a terrible infantile pain. I then went on to experience something that I needed to have experienced in infancy, namely the healing of the wound by being taken back by father, mother, or father-mother love. In extreme infancy one's earthly father or mother is the only form which our Heavenly Father can take. We know of no one beyond them. They are "god." Hence, in the adult mind healing is experienced as coming from the Heavenly Father. The Heavenly Father of adult life *is* the earthly father of extreme infancy.[11]

After an especially painful session he wrote, "Peace and life at last. And through the suffering, peace. It is from father and mother, AND MOTHER, and God. The Virgin is my friend, no longer to shield me from pain—God is the Mother God." [12]

Again, "Now, deep down within me, the mother-child relationship is recovered, the God-child relationship is more real, near, and tender. Because I now know that when she was my only 'giver of life' I could and did securely take it from her—so by the same spiritual machinery I can now rest in Him who is the Lord and Giver of all Life."[13]

D. Trust Illuminative Case

Alberta sought counseling help at a newly formed pastoral counseling center in a small midwestern city. Her stated reason for seeking counseling— loneliness. She was a thirty-one-year-old widowed mother of boys fourteen, eleven, and ten, and a girl seven. Alberta was four feet ten inches in height and one hundred and ninety pounds in weight. She had a few months earlier undergone a major operation to realign her digestive tract in order to bypass a large portion of her intestines to help reduce her obesity. Two years previously her husband had been killed in an auto accident.

At the time she was first seen by a counselor she was struggling with her feelings of infatuation with twenty-year-old Sterling, a fellow member of her church who, though not at all interested in her as a potential mate or even sexual partner, had befriended her and her children by providing rides to and from worship services and other church events. Alberta had never learned to drive.

Third in a siblingship of six children (three boys and three girls) born to a general laborer who married Alberta's mother when he was twenty-five and she was thirteen, Alberta presented a dramatic picture by her person, history, and stated problem. That picture was of a starving individual, hungry for any kind of food, but especially for emotional, mothering, caring kinds of food. Raised by a child mother not much older than she, forced by premarital pregnancy at sixteen into her own problem-laden marriage to a problem drinker, forced by her husband's sudden death to mother her own four children without help, she seemed arrested developmentally within the first year of her life and desperate for adequate mothering.

Alberta's mother-god had related to and interacted with Alberta in such a way as to give her mostly unpleasant, even frightening experiences in that critical first year of life, leaving Alberta unfulfilled at the basic trust versus mistrust level, providing her with strong impressions of the inadequacy of her first god's capability (or even hostile unwillingness) to meet her needs.

If there be truth in this hypothesis, Alberta's desperate reaching out for love (trust) all of her life, her terrible vulnerability, her finally saying in a counseling session, "I need to be needed—I guess that's the big reason I can't say no!" begin to make more sense.

Symbolically her experiences with the institutional expressions of the church (at first Salvation Army, then, later, with Lutheran and Baptist churches) heightened her feelings of helpless, even angry, dependency ("I get so tired of having to ask people for rides every time we need to go to the church!") and her fears that people laugh at her behind her back because she is obese.

In her thinking about finding another husband she would say, "I guess if God intends for me to find a man, it will work out; if he doesn't I'll just have to try to live with it." Her feeling-level lessons about her first god seemed to come to the fore in her talk about God as a heavenly provider who operates by script, or whim, or both, like it or not.

Without excessively verbalizing his stance, the male counselor attempted to provide in small measure some of the good mothering Alberta had been seeking all of her thirty-one years. He made practically no demands whatever in the early meetings and simply tried to convey his feelings of warmth and care to her.

Not surprisingly she quickly found herself eagerly looking forward to each counseling session and freely taking into herself the counselor's care and authority, telling her offending relatives and neighbors in the midst of arguments, "My counselor says for me to. . ." and embarrassedly confessing that her sexual fantasies about Sterling were being replaced by sexual fantasies about her counselor. This confession was heard with appreciation and a word of assurance about the feelings' value. Also, the counselor reminded Alberta of his responsibility to help keep the expression of feeling within a safe, nondestructive, counseling structure.

Thus, in one sense healing had to do with Alberta experiencing the counselor as an authority, i.e., a god of a different sort—one who would love, comfort, even encourage love in return, yet all within relatively safe limits set up for Alberta's protection, a veritable garden of Eden in which she had opportunity to unlearn, in part, the old lessons on the nature of gods.

Only gradually did the counselor begin to encourage Alberta's responsibility taking. First he praised her attempts to pass the state driver's test. Then he gently weaned her away from "My counselor says" toward "I say" in setting appropriate limits for her children, relatives, and neighbors. Finally there came a day of real celebration for both Alberta and the counselor when she shared the news of her purchase of her own car and her budding relationship with an employee of the service station where she stopped for gasoline.

E. Implications for Religious Education

"If there is any one place where the emphasis of the church needs to be placed, it is with the parents of children under six years of age." These words of an established pastoral care authority succinctly point the way toward application of a developmental psychology of religion in practice. Himself convinced of the power of Erikson's insights, Carroll Wise discusses their impact and pushes for greater aid from the church for parents of young children—group-sharing experiences, exposure to developmental didactic material, the tying together of psychological and theological formulations, and provision of adequate pastoral counseling support for particular problems.[14]

Among the twelve tests for mentally healthy religion developed by Howard J. Clinebell, Jr., is the following question. Does a particular form of religious thought and practice strengthen or weaken a basic sense of trust and relatedness to the universe? In his discussion of this question, Clinebell cites Moses' blessing of the people in Deuteronomy 33:27 as an example of how religious expression produces a reaffirmation of the trustworthiness of life and thereby strengthens and heals the personalities of the participants.[15]

At any rate, the significance of the necessity for the church to make meaningful applications of understandings of the nature of human beings, their needs, and their psychosocial-religious development in its overall ministry cannot be overstated.

4

Autonomy and Good and Evil

A. The Specific Hypothesis Elaborated

As we have shown, Erikson sees autonomy as the basic issue in his second stage roughly in the years two, three, and four. Here the psychosocial modalities become to hold on and to let go. This is focused at the other end of the digestive tract from that of stage one, namely, the anal orifice as well as the bladder sphincter. The whole struggle gets dramatized in Western culture by toilet training. What Erikson says is that in the struggle for control between the parents and the child of the conduct of eliminative body functions, the child either learns a sense of his own autonomy, of selfhood; or he fails to so learn and ends up feeling mostly in doubt about his own autonomy as well as ashamed, exposed, and angry about the power of others.

In another dimension I maintain that in the midst of this psychosocial crisis there is also a religious crisis taking place; there are religious feeling-level lessons being learned, specifically about the nature of good and evil. If the parent-gods, the external authority figures, Mommie and Daddy, are sensitive and caring enough about allowing the child to grow and become his own person, they are going to try to provide an environment, an atmosphere in which he or she can understand what the choices are and then freely choose to put feces and urine in the appropriate place, and then choose out of his or her own sense of autonomy to do what he or she is being invited to do over against being ordered, commanded, forced into it prematurely before even perhaps the child has the actual physical control of its sphincters. Of course the baby literally does not have that kind of control. So it is a growing into, a nurturing and inviting process, hopefully, in which the parent-gods convey to the child that he or she is a person of worth even if he or she puts the feces and urine in the wrong places. If the child is condemned and demeaned for this, and if the products of its body that really felt pretty good when they were being passed are condemned and spoken of as horrible and evil, then it is just a small step toward the evils of the product and feelings of worthlessness becoming intertwined. The child may get a feeling that he or she is nothing but a worthless producer of feces. The child may learn that its acts make it what it is and that there is no real sense of separation between being and doing. It largely depends upon how Mommie reacts when Baby defecates on the floor or the bed. Imagine the effect if she screams, "Johnny, you horrible little thing. That's an awful thing to do to Mommie. Now look, Mommie has to clean it up. Good little boys put it in the pot."

Here theological lessons are taking place. Here, as Wayne Oates calls them, many an "unforgiving legalist" has been born, many a person who learns that one must live by rigid, unattainable rules, and those who infringe upon the rules must be destroyed without mercy; the primary value, then, is law and order. Here we have the beginnings of the unrelenting "guardian of the faith," the one-man army who goes out to do battle with the forces of evil in the world. Those who pass this stage without a sense of autonomy find it easy to look at the world and say, "This is good, that is evil. This is white, that is black." Everything in the world fits into a pigeonhole. This is the birthing place of the fundamentalist mind-set. Authority is definitely in focus here, though it is involved in each of the stages. In psychopathology this is also seen as the breeding ground of the obsessive-compulsive individual, the person who tries to deny the chaos he feels by overcontrolling.

Here it is that persons learn at the deepest levels of being whether or not their gods (God?) are basically good, kindly, accepting, whether or not the world is essentially safe, whether or not they can experience their own worth as creatures quite apart from their deeds and misdeeds, and whether or not authority can be exercised in roughly equal amounts from internal and external sources.

B. Religio-Cultural Referents

"God saw all he had made, and indeed it was very good " (Gen. 1:31). "Then Yahweh God gave the man this admonition, 'You may eat indeed of all the trees in the garden. Nevertheless of the tree of the knowledge of good and evil you are not to eat, for on the day you eat of it you shall most surely die'" (Gen. 2:16–17). "Then the serpent said to the woman, 'No! You will not die! God knows in fact that on the day you eat it your eyes will be opened and you will be like gods, knowing good and evil' " (Gen. 3:4–5).

Perhaps it is too bizarre an interpretation to claim that the preceding verses symbolize the toilet training of mankind! Less bizarre is the view that these Scripture verses at the very least represent the first contact mankind had with externally set limits, that the struggle involved the autonomy of mankind, that the outcome was both good and evil.

Good in the sense that mankind did in the process come to a sense of his own autonomy, his own personhood vis à vis the autonomy and the personhood of God.[1] The struggle resulted in a certain new emotional, physical, and spiritual distantiation between mankind and God. "So Yahweh God expelled him from the garden of Eden, to till the soil from which he had been taken" (Gen. 3:23).

Evil in the sense that mankind did in the process come to a sense of shame.[2] "The man and his wife heard the sound of Yahweh God walking in the garden in the cool of the day, and they hid from Yahweh God among the trees of the garden" (Gen. 3:8).

The doctrine of good and evil eventually developed to the point of formulation of the classical question of theodicy. How are we to understand the existence of evil in a world created by a God who is omnipotent and perfectly good? And there the doctrine remains in its development. One theologian has said that theodicy is

41

the rock upon which all theology is shipwrecked. If God cannot stop evil, he is not all-powerful. If God will not stop evil, he is not all good.

Various attempts have been made to cope with this dilemma. One solution is to project the blame for evil upon Satan, demons, evil forces of whatever label. In an excellent survey of the demonology of Israel and surrounding cultures, Edward Langton in part concluded:

1) belief in the existence of evil spirits has prevailed among all the peoples of the world from the earliest times;

2) the concept of Satan was the product of native Hebrew thought, with some Persian influence;

3) Jesus accepted uncritically the Jewish teaching concerning the existence and operations of evil spirits and Satan as the head of the kingdon of evil.

Langton's further observation that these ideas once "near to the centre of the picture have now a place only upon the fringe"[3] is validated by the widespread public appreciation of comedian Flip Wilson's defusing line, "The devil made me buy that dress!"

A second solution to the problem of evil is the simple denial that evil is real. Notable proponents of this solution are Mary Baker Eddy and the practitioners of Christian Science.

All reality is in God and His creation, harmonious and eternal. That which He creates is good, and He makes all that is made. Therefore the only reality of sin, sickness, or death is the awful fact that unrealities seem real to human, erring belief, until God strips off their disguise. They are not true, because they are not of God.[4]

A third solution distinguishes between the natural and the moral and maintains that values of good and evil may be assigned only in the dimension of the moral.

Things themselves have no natural power to form our judgments. . .

If thou art pained by any external thing, it is not this thing which disturbs thee, but thy own judgment about it. . . (we should) judge only those things which are in our power, to be good or bad.[5]

These three attempts to come to grips with the problem of good and evil, plus no doubt intermediate positions, offer unconscious but powerful religio-cultural referent models and precedents for the communication of values of good and evil by parents to their children in the critical years of ages two, three, and four. Autonomy? Shame and doubt? Am I and my products evil? Am I good and my products evil? Am I and my products good? Whichever lesson the child learns is affected by models presented in the religio-cultural milieu.

C. Research Referents

The controlled administration of LSD by Frank Lake to his patients and their ensuing "trips" back into childhood offer one of the very few opportunities to study directly the relationships between autonomy,

43

shame, doubt, good, and evil. Following are excerpts from Lake's transcript taken during LSD sessions with a particular patient. "Why do I get so rigid? All my jaw's constricted. I've never known such disgust and dismay. (He went out to pass water and returned.) . . . all these things are so lacking in sequence, how can there be any organised personality! I feel the personification of evil." Again, five months later,

> I am looking at something pretty horrible, I don't know what it is. A feeling of constriction in the jaw again. I'm getting very frightened. (Returning from a visit to the lavatory he said) Leaking from both ends—disgust with faeces. I've been made to feel disgust at having done something. I'm trying to say, I couldn't help it. (There is an expression of extreme disgust on his face.) 'Oh yes, you could help it.' (He lies with his mouth open in astonishment.) I've been made to feel responsible for living. Fearing terribly. Trying to think it out. Am I guilty? I'm condemned, but what for?

I. J., a married clergyman in his late forties recorded the following.

> I am not mad, but the light is going out. God is the Devil, and the Devil God. Every damn blasted thing I believed in is gone because there is no one left to believe it . . . Only the scornful sneer of the Devil's lips, but they are my lips, my lips against myself. What is the point of anything when you only exist as the echo of Satanic laughter over what was there once. The Devil's sacrament of Death. I am going to it, to eat and drink death . . . to be death. I can't stand much more of this . . . soon I shall be celebrating the Devil's Mass and my own damnation. None can be saved, save they be damned first—but I must join the Devil in damning myself. As if the Devil and I are one composite person. I must join the Devil's laughter against all saving agencies towards me.

Behind the figure of the saved one stands the shadow, what a mighty shadow, of the lost one. I get a fantasy of squirting everything out per bowel and mouth . . . against mother? . . . The faintest detached sort of memory of being spanked for it.[6]

Though excerpted records from the experience of only two individuals, the material bears out startlingly the hypothesis focusing the doctrine of good and evil at Erikson's stage of autonomy versus shame and doubt.

D. Autonomy Illuminative Case

Just home from a circle meeting at a friend's house where the topic discussed over tea, coffee, and cake had been "Which mother has the youngest toilet-trained child and is, therefore, the most competent?" cheeks still pinked by the crisp March air, eyes flashing with resolve, Lucy addressed baby Mark, "Mother wants you to put your peepee and poopoo into this pottie (pointing to a small blue container with two unconcerned baby chicks emblazoned on its side) from now on. I know you can do it for Mother and show her what a fine, good boy you are." Mark looked at Lucy intently, smiled, and wet his pants.

Angry, firm in her knowledge that she was doing the right thing, Lucy spanked Mark sharply several times across his diaper-padded bottom and said loudly, "No, Mark! Shame on you! Good boys tell their mothers when they have to peepee. Then the mothers help get their pants down, and they peepee into the pottie. Now if you don't do it, Mother may have to give such a naughty boy to the garbage men to take away next time they come by!''

These were her exact words, her heard words; what Mark felt was more, was this: "I don't love you anymore and will get rid of you, will destroy you unless you do this business of putting your peepee and your poopoo in a certain place and at a certain time!" Even as it struck chill terror deep in his being, this ultimatum made Mark extremely angry. After the first few accidents and the accompanying spanks and threats, Mark kicked, screamed, and pounded his tiny clinched fists against anything within reach in his blind, all-consuming rage. Part of this rage had its basis in physiological reality; nine-month-old babies have not yet reached the epigenetic pleroma, the fullness of time, in which conscious controls can be exerted from the brain to constrict or relax the crucial sphincter muscles. Thus, desperate fear vied with rabid rage for position as Mark's primary emotion as he experienced the horrible, indescribable loneliness of life without the voice-touch-hold God's love, the hellishness of existence outside the Garden.

Mark's baby mind quickly intuited in its baby way how to cope: "Give the voice-touch-hold God what it wants so I can have what I want." He took his cues. He engaged in accursed work as a lesser evil than his present state. He worked a physiological miracle in his small body through sheer determination of will. He brought his sphincter muscles under the conscious control of his mind. He chose to put his peepee and poopoo in the appropriate place at the appropriate time. And since open expression of rage was also unacceptable to the voice-touch-hold God, he buried his rage deep within himself, the rage stirred by the rape of his soul in which his voice-touch-hold God forced him to choose out of fear, not out of the autonomous pride possible only a year or so later in his developmental history.

And so it was that Lucy, completely unawares, transmitted to her child a sense of shame and doubt about personhood and worth, a deep-seated but necessarily concealed resentment, a primitive longing for a never-to-be-realized return to the wonderful pre-Fall bliss of the Garden.

E. Implications for Religious Education

The central message to parents of children up to the age of five is clear: Remove moralistic bludgeons from toilet training. Some exposure to a developmental psychology of religion and its close relationship with psychosocial development should help sensitive parents discover the profound religious and moral implications of the ways they manage the toilet training of their children.

Classes for young parents and parents-to-be within the context of the religious group are an extremely meaningful pastoral care function and could well include exposure to popular and well-accepted material on physiological and psychological aspects of child development. The Gesell Institute's *Child Behavior From Birth to Ten* by Frances L. Ilg and Louise Bates Ames and *Between Parent and Child* by Haim G. Ginott are examples of economical paperbacks readily available for use in such classes, with excellent material on readiness for bowel and bladder control and matter-of-fact approaches to toilet training. Ginott directly addresses the matter of autonomy and its importance in one section of his book.[7]

Howard Clinebell's third test for mentally healthy religion addresses itself to the autonomy/good-evil issue and directly related problems with authority and dependency.

> Does a particular form of religious thought and practice stimulate or hamper the growth of inner freedom and personal responsibility? Closely related questions are these: Does it encourage healthy or unhealthy dependency relationships—mature or immature relationships with authority? Does it encourage growth of mature or immature consciences?[8]

These and other spin-off issues can and should be approached and seriously dealt with within the structures and programs of the churches if the needs of parents and their children are to be met meaningfully.

5

Initiative and Sin—Redemption

A. The Specific Hypothesis Elaborated

Erikson maintains that in the ages four, five, and six the psychosocial crisis is one in which a child either learns that it is all right to express initiative, to reach out, or that there is something terribly wrong with this drive, and it is something that one should feel guilty about. The psychosocial modality is to make, to make like, to make out. This takes place within the context of the Freudian theory about what happens to people in this age and again assumes a religious dimension. It is here that children are really learning their feeling-level lessons about the nature of sin and what it feels like to be redeemed or cast into outer darkness. They learn by the way parents respond to them as they express their making-out, initiative-taking impulses.

It is totally unacceptable to me as the father-god for my son to take my wife from me. I am not going to let him get away with it. That is a sin within the context of our family. It may be the unforgivable one. So, my task is to convey that to him without destroying him physically, emotionally, and spiritually. I literally have that kind of power. I have the power to cast him into outer darkness, as I think every father has over every son and every mother has over every daughter when the child is only four, five, or six. In the practical working out of this drama, what does a parent do when the child reaches out and tries to take the initiative, to literally take the parent of the opposite sex away from the parent of the same sex? How do we harness this initiative, how do we bless it while unconsciously condemning the object? I think by trying to convey forgiveness, acceptance, redemption. These are the theological terms for very real, vital feelings. It is unacceptable and unforgivable for my son to take my wife away from me, but I have let him live, and he lives now. I love him and let him know the best ways I can just what he can get away with, just what he can express, just what the limits of acceptable behavior are. Gradually I think he has done as Freud predicts and as Erikson has affirmed. When he realized that he couldn't destroy me, he decided to join me. Now he is identifying with me.

Murderous impulses toward the parent that he both loves and hates puts the child in a terrible, awful position. He must hide the unacceptable impulses from himself and from his parent, especially if the parent is very threatened or insensitive to the drama that is being played out. I have worked with patients in the mental hospital situation who are completely obsessed with the idea that they have committed the unforgivable sin. And I have made the naïve mistake with these individuals in thinking that all I had to do was quote them a certain number of Scripture passages or engage with them in debate, that if I were the best debater I could simply convince them that they had not committed the unforgivable sin. But this is on such a deep feeling level that all the scriptural references in the Bible will not reduce the feeling of being cut off. Somewhere along the line in a deep way they have been convinced that they are really worthless, unforgiven, without mercy, and deserve to be burning in hellfire or whatever their imagery of it is. All the Sunday school lessons, all the catechism classes which emphasize that God is love, that God is forgiving, and that there is such a thing in the Christian faith as redemption may fall on deaf ears if a child has at home experienced from his first gods the feeling lessons that he or she is worthless, that he or she has committed the unforgivable sin in whatever ways it has been conveyed. The feeling-level, unconsciously learned lessons about sin and redemption must be appreciated, I find, as such, and furthermore, can only be unlearned or relearned at the same level through a modeling of honest concern.

B. Religio-Cultural Referents

A universal element in religion from the dawn of history has been and is the realization of some kind of estrangement between mankind and the divine.

Totemism, one of eleven common features of primitive religions isolated by Noss and defined by him as a sense of intimate relationship with other orders of life, including even inanimate objects,[1] is seen by Freud as one of mankind's attempts to deal with that estrangement, which is in Freud's view essentially estrangement between father and son. After an elaborate comparison between primitive totems and childhood phobias, Freud concludes that the original totem animal is the father. He then points out that the two central prohibitions of totemism, not to kill the totem and not to have sexual intercourse with a woman of the same totem, are directly analogous with the two crimes of Oedipus, who killed his father and married his mother.[2]

Leaning heavily on the anthropologists of his day and making no claims for exactitude, Freud hypothesized a basic, horrific drama at the dawn of history which provides the primitive basis for the doctrine of original sin, sacramental meals, the sense of guilt, and resulting attempts to expiate that guilt. "One day the brothers who had been driven out came together, killed and devoured their father and so made an end of the patriarchal horde," that group of females which the violent and jealous father had kept for himself while banishing the sons as they came of age.[3]

Later mythological figures reflect the son's efforts to replace the father. Attis, Adonis, and Tammuz, all youthful divinities who enjoyed the favors of mother-gods, were guilty enough to receive punishment via castration and/or death.

Genesis 22:1–19 contains the account of the testing or temptation of Abraham to slaughter his son Isaac as an offering before God. Whatever else the record might commemorate—the testing of the faith of Abraham, the inner struggle of Abraham to demonstrate complete commitment to his God in a culturally accepted manner, the demonstration of progress beyond the primitive and repugnant practice of human sacrifice —whatever else it might mean, the passage is an interesting example of a father who came very close to exercising his power of life and death over his son on the death side, yet allowed the son to live on.

Chapters 15 through 19 of II Samuel record the poignant struggle for power between David the father and Absalom the son. Absalom gathered power and entered the capital city of Jersualem on the heels of his fleeing father, King David. Upon the counsel of his aides, Absalom chose as the ultimate symbolic act of the rebellion's consummation the taking of his father's concubines. "So they pitched a tent for Absalom on the housetop and in the sight of all Israel Absalom went to his father's concubines" (II Sam. 16:22). As the tide of battle turned in David's return to power, David's careful instructions to his captains to spare Absalom's life were disregarded, and Absalom was killed anyway. What might have been a triumphal reentry into the city became an act of mourning during which "The King had veiled his face and was crying aloud, 'My son Absalom! Absalom, my son, my son!'" (II Sam. 19:4).

The ultimate father-son relationship in the Christian context is of course that encompassing God and Jesus Christ. Of this Freud has the following to say.

There can be no doubt that in the Christian myth the original sin was one against God the Father. If, however, Christ redeemed mankind from the burden of original sin by the sacrifice of his own life, we are driven to conclude that the sin was a murder. The law of talion, which is so deeply rooted in human feelings, lays it down that a murder can only be expiated by the sacrifice of another life: self-sacrifice points back to blood-guilt. And if this sacrifice of a life brought about atonement with God the Father, the

53

crime to be expiated can only have been the murder of the father.[4]

This solution to the problem of the significance of the death of Jesus Christ on the cross is strangely akin to and uses similar imagery to the medieval Christian explanation—the satisfaction theory of the Atonement. Here God demands satisfaction for the travesty done to his honor by the sins of mankind; the only act adequate to restore God's honor is of course the sacrificial act of his only begotten Son.

Two contemporary men must be mentioned in this discussion of the religio-cultural referents for the relationship of sin and redemption to the Oedipal struggle—Dietrich Bonhoeffer and Thomas J. J. Altizer. Bonhoeffer, the now near-sainted German pastor-teacher who resisted Hitler and died at the hands of the Nazis mere days before the end of World War II, became the precursor of the death of God as a formal theological position through his agonizing experience.

> The God who makes us live in this world without using him as a working hypothesis is the God before whom we are ever standing. Before God and with him we live without God. God allows himself to be edged out of the world and on to the cross. God is weak and powerless in the world, and that is exactly the way, the only way, in which he can be with us and help us.[5]

It is only a step further to the position brashly announced by Altizer that on the cross God thoroughly emptied himself, he "annihilated" himself as pure being in order to actualize himself in the world, he transmuted entirely his transcendence into immanence.[6] Altizer insists that since Calvary, God is dead, irrevocably surpassed as the empty and alien "Other" who in heavenly isolation stays untouched and unaffected by the world.[7]

This theological stance ties back noticeably to the psychological assessment of Freud that through the Atonement a son religion displaced (murdered?) the father religion, that evidence of this substitution lies in the revival of the ancient totem meal (communion) in which the company of brothers consumes the flesh and blood of the son, no longer the father, and obtain sanctity and identification with the son thereby.[8]

This coming together of psychological and theological assertions at this juncture in history causes the very tentative idea to be formed that perhaps in the developmental life of Western culture-religion this could possibly be the third, Oedipal stage.

C. Research Referents

Freud spoke of the superego as the heir of the Oedipus complex, hypothesizing that a precipitate is formed in the ego by the resolution or outcome of the Oedipal struggle. This precipitate, or modification of the ego, stands in contrast to the other constituents of the ego in the form of "an ego-ideal or superego." [9] Unfortunately, research on the elements in superego formation has barely started.

There is a considerable literature based on clinical observation and largely sympathetic to Freud's theory. This includes the writings and findings of psychoanalysts J. C. Flugel, Heinz Hartmann, Edith

Jacobson, and Freud's daughter Anna, who directed intensive studies of children in the Hampstead Clinic resulting in the Hampstead index on the superego.[10]

Melanie Klein, prominent British child analyst, found clinical data enough to take issue with Freudian theoretical formulations about the superego at the point of *timing*. She maintains that guilt and superego formation occur as early as six months, arising out of infant-mother relationship, not the Oedipal triangle.[11]

Erich Fromm disagrees with Freud regarding the *etiology* of the superego. Whereas Freud sees the superego springing from sexual concerns, Fromm sees the beginnings of conscience in the child's response to power and parental authority.[12]

David Ansubel challenges Freudian superego theory by rejecting the concept as adequate for the understanding of *guilt*. In what Stein describes as "perhaps the most carefully systematized treatment to date" [13] Ansubel draws on the developmental research of Piaget, Gesell, Havighurst, and others to hypothesize that since the ego tests reality and represses socially unacceptable elements of the id, there is no function left to perform, and, therefore, the superego is only mythical.[14]

In recent years the behaviorists have leveled a sharp attack upon Freudian theory in general and upon its applications in treatment in particular. Their thesis is that it is fallacious to assume the so-called medical model and treat "symptoms" of some "underlying complex" produced by complicated "dynamics." Rather, behaviors are taken at face value and seen as the result of conditioning; if one can break down behaviors into small increments and control the variables, one can simply unlearn old behaviors and learn new, more desirable ones. The literature produced by the behaviorists and learning theorists (Mowrer, Wolpe, Eysenck, Skinner, Watson, Jones, Dunlap, Salter, Shoben, Dollard, Miller, and others) is massive and increasing.

Though the behaviorists' data is impressive, Ralph Metzner has raised significant questions about applying learning theory based upon animal experiments to complex human behavior.

> It is noteworthy that the most successful cases of the application of learning theory to treatment have usually involved well-defined, objective, visible behaviour deficits. A general theory would require extensive consideration of (1) how "stimuli" are organized, i. e., of perception, its distortions and idiosyncracies; and (2) how "responses" are organized, i. e., of behavioural sequences, of goals, strategies and interactions.[15]

D. Initiative Illuminative Case

Betty, a reasonably attractive housewife in her midthirties, appeared at the study of a minister shortly after her regular appointment with her psychiatrist. She explained that the minister had been highly recommended by an acquaintance, that the treatment process with the psychiatrist included her husband as well as the children of both spouses from each's previous marriage, that the psychiatrist was an incompetent oaf, and that all the parties involved were ganging up on her and expecting her to do all the therapeutic work, to take all the responsibility for the family's problems.

The minister, puzzled, took a neutral, listening

stance then later discreetly checked with the psychiatrist. The psychiatrist saw her as an extremely difficult patient because of her anger, resistance, and manipulativeness. The minister reluctantly agreed to see Betty after her psychiatric appointments and did so for three meetings while keeping in touch with the psychiatrist to avoid further confusion and being played off against the psychiatrist.

During this period Betty attended a religious service and had an extremely vivid religious experience: While hearing about the spikes driven into Jesus' hands at the Crucifixion, she became deeply moved; all of her own vague sufferings seemed understood; whereas she had been near suicide, now she had a purpose—to do God's will; whereas she had been hurt and let down by every human being she'd ever tried to love, now she mystically felt God's love; whereas she was rejected, now she was saved, redeemed.

She decided to drop the psychiatrist and keep seeing the minister. The minister arranged several joint sessions with Betty, himself, and the psychiatrist, but Betty ended the relationship with the psychiatrist.

There followed a course of a dozen hour-long sessions spread over a five-month period in which the minister learned of Betty's unhappy childhood, a stormy first marriage culminating in a ferocious divorce court battle throughout which Betty struggled to contain murderous impulses toward her estranged husband, and the dissolution of her second, current marriage to a man she depicted as extremely passive and destroyed by the successive deaths of his mother and first wife. Then Betty presented the minister with a note in which she described her sexual attraction for the minister and her willingness to be involved with him at whatever level he wished.

Partly flattered but mostly shocked and repelled by this overture, the minister tried, as kindly as he could, to explain his limits and unwillingness to become sexually involved with Betty. This was the turning point. Betty countered with another letter explaining the overture simply as a test of his intentions. Formal meetings ceased. After a chance meeting in another setting, Betty engaged in an extremely vindictive campaign to demean the minister in notes directly to him. She would write things like: Reject Christ and the power of His Holy Spirit and you will cause your own destruction—Destruction is ahead of you—You are headed for a fall and it isn't too far off—It will come at a time when you feel protected and secure—You will think you have won the battle only to lose the war and you will not have a second chance.

In another note to a second very influential minister she wrote implying that minister #1 had tried to get her under his control by using sex, for the sole purpose of getting close to her so he could further his own career.

What lies at the core of this drive to destroy every man in her life, most of the time successfully? How did such devilish murder attempts on emotional, spiritual, sexual, vocational, and nearly physical levels become clothed in the language of Zion, in God talk? By a twisting of the understanding of her initiative, her aggressiveness, her capacity to make, to make like a loving female, to make out.

Betty somehow won her father-god, somehow never made the identification with mother-god. She found herself thus committing the unforgivable sin of being emotionally wed to Daddy and of doing away with Mommie. To protect her conscience from this horrible truth, her unconscious engaged in a massive, paranoid turnaround in which her task became to destroy every other male, even seeking them out in a seductive Circe syndrome in order to do so—two husbands, several psychiatrists, and especially, symbolically significantly, several ministers. (About influential minister #2 she once said in cold amusement to minister #1, "He follows me around like a little puppy!") The ultimate emasculation will occur when Betty announces she has become an atheist.

E. Implications for Religious Education

Clinebell's fourth test for mentally healthy religion asks whether or not a particular religious system provides effective means of "helping persons move from a sense of guilt to forgiveness?"[16] Church school curricula and discussion group topics for young adults could well include material on the drama occurring in the lives of children in this third, Oedipal stage, with emphasis upon the feeling lessons they are learning through their parents' actions and reactions.

Does Mother succumb to the advances of her five-year-old son in the sense of allowing him to replace Father (her husband) in her deepest loyalties? Can Mother and Father understand these intrusions and lovingly set limits for the child secure in their relationship with each other? Can Father deal with the "sin" of his five-year-old son without destroying the son on the altar of uncontrolled anger via physical or emotional abuse? That is, can Father forgive his son, let him live, redeem him? If not, the child's inability to comprehend such terms as forgiveness and redemption in his own religious education beyond the merest superficiality can be expected. If so, the child will have experienced his first profound feeling-level lessons in the matters of sin, sins, forgiveness, salvation, redemption.

6

Industry and Works

A. The Specific Hypothesis Elaborated

Erikson's fourth stage is a psychosocial crisis in which he maintains that the lesson to be learned or that fails to be learned is one concerning industry, that an unfortunate resolution of this crisis results in an ongoing feeling in an individual of inferiority. In the religious dimension, the feeling-level lesson to be learned or that fails to be learned in the life of the individual has to do with the doctrine of works. Where does work fit into the scheme of things, as we call it in the theological jargon, "works"? This raises all kinds of spin-off questions.

Are we saved by works, or are we saved by grace? What is the meaning of the rhythm of work and rest? Is work something that is to be seen as good or evil? Erikson says that primitive feelings are at the surface during the earlier stages, e.g., in the battle for control of the child's body and his struggle for autonomy and in the reaching out for the parent of the opposite sex with all the danger and fear of reprisals and the castration fears which are involved. All of that strong, sharp feeling tends to subside in this stage. Things level off, smooth out. Not that these feelings are completely dissipated, never to be seen again. They are shelved for a while, and the child's world now expands outside the family and even outside the immediate neighborhood to the school. Here is a whole new environment, a whole new situation in which the emphasis is on learning the technology of our culture and society.

Erikson believes that there is a school even in the cultures where there are no school buildings. In any society some adult comes along and teaches the child the arts and crafts of the culture that he needs to learn not only to survive but to gain a certain amount of pleasure and worth. For our particular Western civilization we have an institution. The institution is the school. At school the child is exposed to the rigors and disciplines of the three r's as well as to the closely structured shaping of his interpersonal relationships and works in the group. He very quickly learns what is expected and what is intolerable, learns which behaviors cannot be tolerated in the social situation. He is also in the business of learning how to produce things.

Hopefully, he has developed enough of a sense of trust (his parent-gods have given him a feeling of trustworthiness), he has enough of a sense of his own autonomy (his authority-gods have nurtured autonomy in him), he has learned that it is not terrible to reach out and try to make (his urges and impulses have been channeled in ways that are not too frightening to him), to the extent that when he gets to school he has the foundation on which to build and to learn. He can make things, complete the job, get a certain amount of satisfaction out of achieving, out of accomplishing a task.

If along the way these other layers are shaky, if he had trouble at the level of trust with his first gods, if he got hung up on his own autonomy and is not really comfortable in the sense of what is good and what is evil, if he has an extra layer of guilt that he picked up during his Oedipal struggle, if he has failed to make the identification with his model of what adults are supposed to be, of what daddies and mommies are supposed to be, of male and female, then his chances of becoming comfortable with the technological elements like grasping a pen and pencil and learning how to use them, his competence, is really going to be in jeopardy, and he is very likely to come through this period of the elementary school grades feeling inferior, feeling at the religious level that people are really saved by works and that if he cannot work very well, he is therefore lost.

B. Religio-Cultural Referents

Genesis 3:17–19 reads in part:

Because you listened to the voice of your wife and ate from
the tree of which I had forbidden you to eat,
"Accursed be the soil because of you.
With suffering shall you get your food from it
every day of your life.
It shall yield you brambles and thistles,
and you shall eat wild plants.
With sweat on your brow
shall you eat your bread,

until you return to the soil,
as you were taken from it.
For dust you are
and to dust you shall return" (Gen. 3:17–19).

On the other hand the principle of activity, according to Hegel, whereby "the workman has to perform for his subsistence," gives man a dignity consisting "in his depending entirely on his diligence, conduct, and intelligence for the supply of his wants. In direct contravention of this principle" are "pauperism, laziness, inactivity."[1]

Thus, the two examples represent two opposite religio-cultural referents on the essential nature of work and works. The first sees work as a curse. The second sees work as a blessing.

Somewhere in between these two poles, and taking seriously both the curse and the potential for good of work and works, is the greatly influential view of Reformation theologian John Calvin (1509–1564). In his *Institutes of the Christian Religion* he set forth his views. Man, originally good and capable of obeying God's will, lost his goodness and power through Adam's fall and is now absolutely incapable of goodness. Thus, no work of man's has any merit; all men are in a state of ruin meriting damnation. From this hopeless situation some men are undeservedly rescued through the saving work of Jesus Christ who paid the penalty due for the sins of those for whom he died. That work becomes some men's personal possession through the work of the Holy Spirit. Those receiving this possession through repentance and faith then engage in works pleasing to God as *proof* of their saving relationship to Jesus Christ. " 'We are justified not without, and yet not by works.' "[2]

Max Weber's *The Protestant Ethic and the Spirit of Capitalism* recounts the growing relationship between capitalism, which had its roots in the Renaissance, and protestantism, which was strongly shaped by Calvinism. This emerging Calvinist-capitalistic work ethic, coupled with the American pioneer spirit, helped produce the current gigantic technological megalith about which one U.S. comedian has "boasted," to wit, the United States has the grossest national product in the world! Reinforcing and subtly intertwining with this drive toward technological accomplishment was (and is) the American folk-cultural religion which preaches the demand for more and more works, even when the work seems to be all done, and produces guilt in one when one is not diligently at work.[3]

As Annie L. Coghill (1836–1907) taught us to sing even after leading us through verses about the "morning hours" and the "sunny noon,"

Work, for the night is coming,
Under the sunset skies;
While their bright tints are glowing,
Work, for daylight flies.
Work till the last beam fadeth,
Fadeth to shine no more;
Work while the night is darkening,
When man's work is o'er.

Currently we see the youth culture acting out its rage against the Calvinist-capitalistic work ethic by simply refusing to affirm these values. It looks at the values that are handed down and rejects them. Wayne Oates, a professor of pastoral care in a Baptist seminary, has written a book, *Confessions of a Workaholic,* and finds that it is on the best seller list. Why? Because this touches us, and we must consider that deep down inside we have learned a lesson that we are really nothing unless we have good works to show or a certain amount of wealth accumulated. Walk up to somebody on the street or in some public place or conveyance and ask, "Who are you?" and the chances are you will get an answer in terms of that individual's vocation. "I'm a plumber," or "A doctor," or whatever.

Many of us in my generation have a real hangup with leisure. As a minister I have gotten many subtle signals out of the folk-culture religion of my particular background that to sit down, to relax, to rest is basically to be vulnerable to some criticism by a member of the congregation. The minister often finds himself suffering a fishbowl existence in which there is no time off, no place to hide, as the psalmist complained. The expectation of God, the people, and the minister himself seems to be one of continuous good works, around-the-clock, superhuman effort to minister to the souls. After a while this messianic model gets tremendously oppressive and is one of the vocational hazards and hassles of many a minister. To compound the problem, this hangup is almost unavoidably conveyed onto the very people to whom the individual is trying to minister.

No wonder Harvey Cox finds eager readers for his book, *The Feast of Fools,* in which the question is raised, "Whatever happened to the festival, the celebration called 'The Feast of Fools'?'' Somehow the Calvinist-capitalistic work ethic squeezed that out of the Christian calendar. One little vestige of it remains in America in the form of the Mardi Gras just before Lent; and New Orleans is about the only place I know of where people have it as a ritual with at least a quasi blessing from the church to go out and have a good time, to enjoy, to have fun, to put on a mask and act crazy and silly. As I understand it, a few hundred years ago during the Feast of Fools people could actually dress up like the king and mock him and make fun of him and get rid of some of their pent-up anger and their problems with the authority of the king. It was built in, it was affirmed, it was blessed as a ritual. But not anymore.

And now our very technological competence is moving us toward the four-day workweek and extensive leisure time. Hopefully, we can relearn our feeling-level theological lesson regarding the place of works in creation before our leisure drives us crazy as a culture. (Could our compulsive, massive rushing in expensive vehicles to camping areas even more congested than our neighborhoods during leisure time be a symptom of our culturally crazy attempts to manage our hangups with the doctrine of works?)

C. Research Referents

The sociology of religion has recently been taken to task for its research efforts which for the most part have identified religiosity with institutionalized religious conduct. To the list of causative factors (philosophical roots in logical positivism, convenience, and attempts to satisfy denominational sponsors)[4] should be added the indirect but powerful effect of a works-oriented religio-cultural base.

A clear example of the subtle influence of the works orientation in religious research can be seen in a study titled "Measuring the Religious Variable: Replication." This project builds on the efforts over some twenty years of such researchers as Allport, Fichter, Glock, Lenski, Wilson, Faulkner, DeJong, Whitam, and Pittard by confirming earlier findings that correlational techniques can identify clearly separate dimensions existing within the religious variable. "Ten scales, defining different dimensions of religious *behavior* and *congregational involvement*, were developed " (italics mine).[5]

What is pertinent to this discussion of the impact on religious research of a works-oriented religio-cultural milieu is a close look at the items grouped under the ten headings (creedal assent, devotionalism, church attendance, organizational activity, financial support, religious knowledge, growth and striving, extrinsic, salience-behavior, and salience-cognition).[6]

Of the fifty-four items extracted by correlational and factor-analysis techniques (five items appeared in two of the headings), one dealt primarily with feeling, eight related to religious knowledge, eight to religious belief, and thirty-seven were works-oriented. Thus, 68.5 percent of the items factored out concerned some form of religious activity, reflecting the heavy weight placed upon religious works and justifying Luckmann's criticism.[7]

D. Industry Illuminative Case

Phyllis, a twenty-nine-year-old, short, chubby, dark-haired, rapid speaking, married mother of girls aged six and one, sought counseling help for what she termed "personal and marital concerns." She had grown up in a large city with her two-years-younger sister and eight-years-younger brother, the family of a Jewish fireman and his wife (a convert from Roman Catholicism to Judaism).

The parents' marriage Phyllis rated as very unhappy; there was very little communication, and no tenderness, no touching. Phyllis' mother lost herself in work around the house, putting all of her energy into doing things like making beds, cooking meals, keeping things orderly, and above all, keeping busy. "Busy people are happy people" and "Idle hands are the devil's workshop" were more than adages, they described her lifestyle, and she thoroughly indoctrinated Phyllis at a profound level. Phyllis' mother-god tied worth and works together so inexorably that Phyllis' sense of trust, autonomy, and initiative took second place to her frantic effort to please and earn recognition by her good deeds.

Unfortunately, Phyllis' every attempt failed in that Mother would still not be satisfied, still could not convey warmth or appreciation no matter how hard Phyllis worked. She only demanded more.

Exhausted and enraged, Phyllis sought love elsewhere than at home. After several awkward affairs, Phyllis became pregnant out of wedlock. Not surprisingly, she elected to carry the child to full term, to do the work of childbearing, and to keep the child, the product of her labor.

Then Phyllis met John, a quiet, even withdrawn individual, himself the product of an emotionally arid family climate. John related better to machines than to people and found some vocational satisfaction in his work on machinery. He was totally inept and inexperienced sexually when he met Phyllis. Phyllis took on the task of educating him, of helping him to learn to perform. Again, not surprisingly, she felt disappointment and a lack of pleasure when at last her instructions succeeded and John was able to function more or less adequately.

By the time she arrived at the counselor's office seeking help, John had legally adopted the first child, and they had one "of their own." But Phyllis was growing increasingly intolerant of John's lethargy (by her standards), his lack of aggressiveness in advancing his cause at work (by her standards) and his fantasy of just being a bum.

She was caught in a frantic flurry of activities in which she held down a part-time job and kept the two children and the household at the same high maintenance standard she had had before becoming employed. She resisted attempts by John to get her to slow down, to give up her job, even to go out to dinner with him occasionally. She acknowledged difficulty with touching—avoiding it with her family and defending against it by compulsive work.

In counseling, her continuous barrage of words (another form of work?) was heavily laden with self-deprecating statements indicating strong feelings of inferiority. No wonder that before the third interview she brought in cups, saucers, and some towels. She stated that she noticed the inadequacy of the cups and saucers in use and the complete absence of towels. Symbolically, she was expressing her feelings and seeking recognition, yes, even salvation, in the only way she knew—by work, by good works.

The counselor's own task became one of directly and indirectly challenging her basic life premise, her theological feeling-level assumption about herself, i.e., I am worthless apart from good works and not too convinced of my worth even with good works.

He did this by trying to interpret to her her behaviors and their meanings in his eyes, especially with regard to acts, to works. He did this also by picking up on and affirming with her her strengths apart from things to do—her quick mind, her extraordinary sense of humor, the strength that enabled her to see her need and to reach out for help. He did this by trying to help her learn a new theological lesson at the feeling level: By grace are ye saved through faith, and that not of yourselves. It is the gift of God, lest any man should boast.

E. Implications for Religious Education

The institutional expressions of religion in the United States tend to verbally and intellectually proclaim salvation by grace on the one hand and demand on the feeling and activity levels salvation by works. (You're okay and I'm okay, but you might not be if you don't participate in the church program.) The primary implication of this schizophrenogenic double message is the probability of a full-blown schizophrenic reaction in the institution itself.

Religious educators could well take their cues from the section of Wayne Oates' book, *Confessions of a Workaholic*, entitled "The Religious Outlook of the Converted Workaholic." Cue number one: the nurturing of a forgiving attitude among people regarding standards of competence and the cultivation of patience vis-à-vis intolerance. Cue number two: the development of a sense of irony and humor, a certain ability to be objective about one's hangups, mistakes, and idiosyncrasies to the point of being able to pull back and laugh at oneself and with others. "This irony and humor spring from a person's new awareness that God's acceptance is freely given and not earned by the sweat of one's brow." Cue number three: the rediscovery of a sense of wonder and awe about nature, persons, and activity for pleasure's sake. Cue number four: a deprogramming of corporate worship by those in places of religious leadership from deferred hopes and gratification toward actualization and realization in the present tense.[8]

7

Identity and Man

A. The Specific Hypothesis Elaborated

The fifth psychosocial stage or crisis is the one in which Erikson says the struggle is for identity, with failure resulting in identity diffusion or role confusion. In our religious overlay of Erikson's scheme I am hypothesizing that the religious doctrine in focus at this stage is the doctrine of man, the doctrine of humankind.

Erickson sees this as a stage in which the peer group is extremely important. The related elements of the social order are what he calls ideological perspectives with important implications in the religious dimension. The psychosocial modality is to be, to be oneself. I think of Shakespeare's famous line which, in a real sense, sums up this stage: "To be, or not to be—that is the question."

A part of the struggle here has to do with the individual getting acquainted with specific sexuality. We have looked at Freud's theory that there is a general sexuality emerging during the Oedipal stage. Here it obviously becomes quite specific as the individual moves nearer adult genitality and has to adjust to having an adult body with all its capabilities, with all the potential for joy and pleasure as well as for some destructive aspects. It is believed by Freudians and neo-Freudian psychologists that the Oedipal conflict is reopened at this point with the surging forth of specific sexual feelings, that in a sense the boy now has even more frightening impulses toward his mother, and the girl is again in a fresh and even greater way attracted to her father or father figure.

Another issue is involved—dependence-in-dependence. The person who was totally dependent at the start is gradually becoming more independent in physical skills and emotional awareness of himself as a person. He or she now really has significant power. That is, the adolescent has access to enough money, has acquired the skill to drive, and has learned enough about the world and its workings to be independent. If the impulse overtakes the adolescent to run away, he or she does in fact have the physical and mental capabilities to do so.

There is a struggle between total dependence and total independence. Most of the time the person is somewhere in the middle in a state which I call interdependence. This struggle for independence is not a smooth one and is often a source of stress and pain in the family, especially if the family members are not cognizant of the issues of adolescence, especially if the parents see their task as somehow to keep their child a child and to resist the efforts of the budding adult to push and reach out, to experiment with some emotional, spiritual, and physical distance between himself and the parent.

The peer group at last seems to replace the parent

figures as the major source of external authority, of what to do, what's in, what's out, what to wear, what values are important, what records, what tastes, what movies, whatever idols are to be admired and emulated.

One of the ideological areas has a special importance in the emerging understanding of the nature of the doctrine of man. The individual begins to realize that his or her religion has been a hand-me-down religion. I do not mean to imply by that in any sense that there is anything wrong with hand-me-downs in the imagery of big brother tossing off clothes to little brother. Religion and its expression (or lack of expression) simply is one of the gifts that a parent gives the child as a part of who they are, what they believe, and how they live. A part of the struggle for independence includes the specific religious issue; an adjunct to the "Who am I?" is "Do I really believe what I have been given and taught that I should believe? Is this religious expression or lack of it by my parents mine, or is it theirs?"

Often we see the battle for independence waged on theological grounds, on religious territory. If the adolescent has a particular bent to matters religious, has been especially involved in the church, and is at the same time needing to act out his or her independence, the acting out could easily take the form of choosing another religious expression, wanting to change denominations, wanting to do something different, wanting to reject some of the family's sacred and time-honored beliefs. Not that when an adolescent chooses another religious expression that it is merely and only rebellion. This is the time in which the developing intellect can seriously begin to conceptualize and get in touch with which ideas make sense, which belief systems seem to fit. To change churches or to drop a church relationship can be both independent acting out as well as a serious response to the emerging new conceptualizing capacity the person has.

Sooner or later a developing individual must somehow reconsider the given religious heritage, must be able to look back and sift through, must choose for himself so that it becomes a first-hand, chosen religious expression.

Adolescence is the time in our technological culture when vocational and educational decisions have to be made. And it seems that they are having to be made earlier and earlier in the educational process. When does one have to decide if one really wants to be a doctor? Quite early in terms of the prerequisites.

The central, core issue for adolescence is "Who am I? What does it mean to be a human being? What does it mean to be a female human being over against male human being? Where do I fit in the scheme of things? Am I my own god, or is there a greater authority?"

If I find myself, for example, as a male adolescent, strongly attracted to my male friends and even discover some specifically sexual stirrings in me toward them, does that mean that I have to take on the label of homosexual, or do so-called normal males have these stirrings within them at times? When I look at supposedly female attributes and find some of them fitting me, although I know that I have the male physical equipment and have been taught that means I am a male, am I to be threatened and panic, or am I to somehow integrate that into my idea of what it means to be a man? The converse is true for the female. What are the parameters of masculinity and femininity? Where and how do we discover what it means to be human and to be sexual human beings?

B. Religio-Cultural Referents

What does it mean when I read in Genesis 1:26–28 that I have been created in the image of God? Does that mean that God is up there somewhere with arms and legs and face and a voice, or does it mean something else? What do I do with Psalm 8? When I look at this magnificent, vast expanse of the universe I have to ask myself what am I, and yet I am created a little lower than the angels; yet I have been put in charge of the beasts of the field, the fish of the sea, the birds of the air? Where do I fit?

On the one side there are those who say in the name of religion that human beings are basically good and worthwhile. There are others who believe that human beings are basically evil, despicable creatures who are worthless and nothing. Each adolescent has to deal at least superficially if not in a profound way with which view checks out with his or her perception of reality, personal nature, and the nature of the people he or she knows.

Rituals help people in their passage through this stage of life. For the Jewish male it is the bar mitzvah, a religious ceremony which says, "Today you are a man. Today you get a voice in the decision-making process and in the fellowship." For some Christians the ritual is confirmation, a particular rite in which one formally receives the status of an adult in the life of the church. For other Christians it is the act in which an individual makes what is called a profession of faith. One walks down the aisle at an appointed time, at a particular season of the year, in a particular time of the worship service. One pronounces certain formulas that are accepted by the group, and then one is baptized. This is a ritual that is at least in part a rite of passage, a symbolic affirmation that says, "You are moving from the world of childhood to the world of adulthood."

These rituals seem to be losing some of their meaning. This is a natural process. Symbols tend to lose their significance, and new symbols have to develop, to evolve. About the only ritual that society has left is the ritual of the car keys when Dad says to his daughter or son, "Here are the keys. Go to it." That is about the only way left in our prolonged Western adolescence that really gives anybody any kind of a signal that you really have become something more than a child.

The baccalaureate service once had meaning. Many now challenge the ritual of graduation as the feeling that something significant has been completed, dissipates. Are these rituals to be seen as stifling and stupid, or are they helpers to expedite passage into a new stage? For some the battle for independence is being waged and answers to "Who am I?" are being discovered as they consider whether or not to use that time-honored ritual, the marriage ceremony, as one which is meaningful and helpful as opposed to one which is stifling, oppressive, and stultifying.

In a wider cultural sense the identity crisis of contemporary youth is unique, despite the reality that adolescence has always been seen as an intermediary stage of the alternately invigorating and confusing leaving of an overdefined past for the yet unidentifiable future. This uniqueness is twofold.

On the one hand is the uniqueness of quantity. There are simply more youth in the world than ever before in the history of the world. And they now, generally, physically mature earlier and are better informed by a common literacy and a common imagery of mass communication about world conditions.

On the other hand is the uniqueness of power. Youth have linked themselves in their developmental stage with the economic state of the poor and the political state of the underdeveloped in what Erikson calls a "Revolt of the Dependent." He sees youth asking:

> ... when, if not now, in this post-ideological period in history and before cosmic technocracy takes over altogether, will man attempt to combine his timeless values, his new insights, and his coming mastery in one all-human outlook and planning; and who if not they, the young people assembled in the prolonged moratorium of academic life, will live and rebel for the sake of that outlook?

Erikson sees the legitimacy of violence as the greatest single issue in the ideological struggle of today's youth.[1] Whether or not contemporary youth can and/or will incorporate biblical insights and recent theological interpretations (Teilhard de Chardin—man in evolution, Soren Kierkegaard—existential man; Martin Buber—man in dialogue; Reinhold Niebuhr—man as sinner) of the nature of mankind into a meaningful nondestructive new understanding remains to be seen.[2]

C. Research Referents

One important question for which religious research may provide meaningful responses, if not clear-cut answers, relating to the identity-doctrine-of-mankind crisis is: What is the optimal age for the confirmation of youth into full church membership? During a research year in 1962–63 and the two following years, Charles William Stewart became involved in the Normal Development Project, a fourteen-year-old longitudinal study of sixty normal persons then at the stage of early adolescence. Dr. Stewart, Professor of Pastoral Theology and Supervised Ministries at Wesley Theological Seminary, Washington, D.C., attempted in his research to center in upon the religious needs, expressions, and problems of the youth in the overall study.

Using first a pilot study of six youth and then a wider group of twenty-four more, he and the other investigators employed extensive interviews, the Godin Religious Projective Test, a Q-sort test about God concepts, a Likert-type God-concept scale, and a hymn selection test designed to explore emotional needs satisfied in a religious experience.[3]

Although his sample was small and Stewart seems to ignore the research principle that no inference about the total population should be made from sample data without a statistical analysis, his conclusion is at the very least interesting. "Confirmation in church membership may better be phased to the adolescent's identity crisis." Again, "The study definitely points to holding membership classes later than have been held, preferably in the ninth and tenth grades."[4]

A second important question growing out of adolescent issues to which religious research has addressed itself is: In what way do the churches assist adolescents in channeling their emerging specific sexuality? J. Conrad Glass, Jr., asked three hundred and one United Methodist teenaged church leaders to respond to a questionnaire on premarital sex standards. Of the two hundred eighty valid responses, thirty-three percent picked "petting with affection" (the furthest males or females are allowed to go is petting, and this can be done only when there is strong affection present). Sixteen percent chose "nonequalitarian" (males would be given more freedom in regard to kissing and petting, but females would be restricted somewhat; premarital intercourse is considered wrong for both sexes). Ten percent selected "reverse nonequalitarian" (females would be given more freedom in regard to kissing and petting, but males would be restricted somewhat; premarital intercourse is considered wrong for both sexes).[5]

Glass compared his findings with those of other recent studies: Ehrmann (1969) and Reiss (1961) found most teen-aged males upholding the "double standard-orthodox" (males are allowed full sexual relations; females are not) and most teen-aged females choosing "petting with affection." Glass's survey of the literature suggests that sex attitudes are changing in the direction of "permissiveness with affection" (both males and females may have full sexual relations when strong affection is involved) in the data gathered by Freedman (1965), Pope and Knudson (1965), Reiss (1960, 1966, 1967, 1970, 1971), and Smigel and Seiden (1968). However, Reiss (1967), Lindenfield (1960), Heltsley and Broderick (1969), and Bell and Chaskes (1970) have shown that religious activity, and in particular church attendance, has been negatively related to sexual permissiveness.[6]

D. Identity Illuminative Case

Lucy, a fourteen-year-old girl, was admitted to the adolescent unit of a large state mental hospital from a general hospital where she had been treated for severe malnutrition. Her parents had been divorced when she was five, and she had lived with her fashion consultant mother and her two-years-younger brother ever since. She was an active member of a large city Christian church, regular in attendance, and avid in her reading of religious literature. Unsure of her mother's love, torn by her father's attempts to lure her toward him, rejected by peers, denying her budding feminity, she refused to go to school and, ultimately, to eat. Upon her admission she was out of contact with reality, quite emaciated, and expressed three religious ideas: (1) the end of the world is at hand; (2) the second coming of Christ is near; (3) she had conceived of the Holy Spirit and was to give birth to a child in a virgin birth.

Because of the prominence of religious ideation, I became the unit staff's choice for primary therapist. Almost from her admission she began to respond out of her latent strengths and her shock at being sent to the state hospital for treatment. This process is described under the basic eleven headings of Robert Leslie in his book, *Jesus and Logotherapy*, an adaptation of the work of Viktor Frankl to Christian pastoral care.

1. *Exploring height psychology.* Lucy had been disturbed long enough before admission to have been treated by several therapists. She knew the language of depth psychology, but had built up a strong resistance to probes into her unconscious life. Fortunately, she was quite deeply involved in an effort to relate what was happening to her to the God-dimension. A phrase which came to her in the midst of her out-of-contact period and which I urged her to retain even after her furlough was "God is love, love is God." We never pressed the literal meaning of this. There never seemed to be a need to do so. It was there. It was a touchstone. We kept it there.

2. *Mobilizing the defiant power of the human spirit.* Within that thin body rested defiant power. We discovered together that one of the meanings of the refusal to eat had to do with the fact that Lucy's mother put a great deal of emphasis upon "cleaning your plate." What better way, then, to defy her mother's authority? Once Lucy could put this into words, it was almost easy for her to put this energy to work for a more constructive purpose—getting out of the hospital.

3. *Finding the personal life task.* At least one element of Lucy's reason-for-being before hospitalization was to somehow become the savior of her parents'

marriage. In our conversations I spoke to the inappropriateness of this as a task for any child to undertake. She saw this immediately and gradually moved toward the assumption of a more realistic task—being a teenager about to become a woman.

4. *Filling the existential vacuum.*The move toward assumption of the task of becoming a woman was gradual because of her struggle with the question, "Is it worth it?" I find it difficult to describe what occurred in our relationship at this point, but I believe it has to do with most-often-unspoken warmth and hope I had for her and somehow conveyed to her. It amounted to a strong "Yes, it's worth it!" from me to her.

5. *Resolving value conflicts.* No child ought to have to choose which parent to live with, but Lucy did. At least emotionally. We talked about the alternatives, and she finally decided that she needed her mother most. Once this decision was made, a good bit of energy was made available for other things.

6. *Actualizing the self in responsible commitment.* Early in her hospitalization Lucy decided that no matter how rough it had been at home, home was better than the adolescent ward. Once committed to "getting home," she became more willing to try the things which would help her get home: go to school (thus helping her deal with her fears of school); eat (thus literally actualizing her body potential); and make friends (once she made the first effort, this became almost easy).

7. *Realizing creative values*. Another meaning of her refusal to eat was her effort to deny her budding femininity. "If I'm skinny, I won't have to worry about my body having curves!" "Does this work?" "No, not really." Soon she began to talk about getting a kitten, and later I received a photo of that obvious and beautiful symbol of femininity.

8. *Realizing experiential values*. Midway through her hospital stay her mother visited. They simply walked among the trees and enjoyed the day and each other. Lucy spoke later of this visit joyously as her beginning to get acquainted with her mother.

9. *Realizing attitudinal values*. Almost before I could ask, "Do you want to get well?" Lucy was responding out of her shock at being so close to death, "Yes!" This attitude was the one most conducive fact in her rapid comeback.

10. *Restoring man's dignity*. My most anxious time with Lucy was our first meeting. She was out of contact and sitting on her bed. While I was there just briefly, she kept trying to put another pair of pajama pants on over the ones she was wearing, and I kept fearing she would take them both off. By our second meeting she was fully dressed and able to walk with me to my office. I was so relieved to see her basic modesty and human dignity restored that I praised her mightily for her progress. In retrospect I realize that in that first meeting I had been almost grimly determined to treat her as if she were acting in a dignified way, or at least

to convey respect for her as a person created in the image of God. Somehow she got the message.

11. *Exercising man's freedom.* From the first hours of her hospitalization Lucy was able to choose her attitude toward her predicament. From the first that attitude was one of horror at the way her own behavior had brought her very near death and into the state hospital. From this attitudinal stance she began to exercise her freedom to choose behaviors which would move her toward her immediate goal of getting out of the hospital.[7]

E. Implications for Religious Education

Howard Clinebell's sixth test for mentally healthy religion asks the question, "Does a particular form of religious thought and practice handle the vital energies of sex and aggressiveness in constructive or repressive ways?" As Clinebell points out in his discussion, when these drives are labeled as bad, persons must either deny their existence or bear an unnatural burden of guilt feelings. "A positive Christian view of sex holds that it is God-given, to be used appropriately, as any of God's gifts. Christians (and others) should thank God that he devised such an enjoyable way of continuing the race."[8]

An important implication for religious education of the adolescent in the struggle to discover the nature of manhood and womanhood, of identity as an adult person, has to do with the ability of the churches to allow room for rebellion. How much of the developmentally necessary adolescent acting out, in terms of boycotting traditional activities such as worship services and Sunday school, can the churches' leadership tolerate and even appreciate? Can the established leadership make creative use of the often idealistically motivated but painfully accurate criticisms leveled by angry youth?

These questions can be answered in the affirmative to an increasing degree in direct proportion to an increasing sensitivity on the part of church leadership to the developmental issues and struggles of youth and an increasingly focused modeling of what the religiously mature man and woman can be like.

8

Intimacy and Christology

A. The Specific Hypothesis Elaborated

Erikson's sixth stage is the one in which he says the struggle is to attain intimacy. Failing in that striving, one becomes basically isolated from one's fellow human beings. Another term that Erikson uses is "intimacy versus distantiation," or distance. The primary theological doctrine in focus at this stage is Christology. Among the other roles and functions of Jesus Christ is the model that he offers in terms of his accomplishment of being sure enough of his own identity that he could be intimate with a whole range of individuals, be close to them without losing his own identity even though it cost him his life.

Erikson defines intimacy as "the capacity to commit oneself to concrete affiliations and partnerships and to develop the ethical strength to abide by such commitments, even though they may call for significant sacrifices and compromises." Those involved in this process are what he calls partners in friendship, sex, competition, and cooperation. He says the psychosocial modality here is to lose and find oneself in another. The basic virtue learned is love. The basic question is how to get close enough to love, to fight, to achieve without getting lost or getting isolated. How do you give to another without giving it all away? How do you achieve true genitality? How do you achieve inter-dependence? How do you make concrete commitments involving sacrifice while achieving relatively guilt-free satisfaction of basic human needs? By finding a certain amount of self-esteem in just being a person, having some ability to cope with life and its stresses, achieving some meaningful interpersonal relationships, finding the basic hunger and sex drives being satisfied, and finding a certain amount of purpose and meaning, a certain amount of significance in life.[1]

Out of a very difficult process that took hundreds of years, there was hammered out what is known as the orthodox solution to the christological problem. At the Council of Chalcedon the church fathers said, "We, then, following the holy Fathers, all with one consent, teach men to confess one and the same Son, our Lord Jesus Christ, the same perfect in Godhead and also perfect in manhood; truly God and truly man, of a reasonable soul and body; consubstantial with the Father according to the Godhead, and consubstantial with us according to the manhood, in all things like unto us, without sin."[2]

A book by William Pittenger entitled *The Word Incarnate* updates the language of the orthodox christological solution and makes it more meaningful to moderns.

The Eternal Son or Word so appropriated and employed the humanity which by divine providential operation was conceived and born of Mary that he possessed in that humanity an organ for self-expression which was adequate to his purposes, while the human life which was conceived and born of Mary so appropriated and expressed the Eternal Son or Word that such an organ was in fact available for the Son's or Word's purposes among men.[3]

This God/man potential that was actualized in the person of Jesus Christ is also potential in every human being. What really makes Jesus Christ different from other humans in this view is that he completely actualized himself in his identity and thereby somehow bridged the gap between the temporal and the eternal, the divine and the human, the ordinary and the special.

Accordingly, then, you and I in our better moments, our most turned-on, enriched moments, achieve this fullness, this intimacy with another human being in relationship. I see this as very close to what Erikson is saying when he talks about intimacy. I do not mean to imply as did Thomas a Kempis and Charles M. Sheldon that the idea is to imitate Christ and become pathetic little Jesus puppets, unrealistically trying to mimic what for him was quite real.

Once a few years ago I preached a sermon on the imitation of Christ and got carried away with Charles M. Sheldon's *In His Steps*. As soon as I got out of the service and headed for home I found myself in a crisis. On my usual stop to buy the Sunday paper I was forced to face the fact that the big issue in the book was absurd to me. I had gotten into the trap of looking at the life of Christ and thinking that I had to become a rubber stamp formed in that precise mold. I learned that day that I am different from Charles M. Sheldon, Thomas a Kempis, and Jesus Christ.

What I am trying to say now is quite different. Of all the stages and attempts to weave into the life crises theological issues, this may be the most complex and difficult to conceptualize.

Each of us is given a certain set of capabilities, a certain set of genetically inherited possibilities. Each of us is a person unique from all the rest of humanity. As one is able to get in touch with his potential, as one is able to discover his unique identity, then from that base, one is increasingly able to reach out to other human beings and in his best moments becomes fully human. In those moments one is in his unique way fully related to the divine. Not in the same personal style that Jesus Christ related to the divine, but in the same proportion of potential actualized in intimacy.

In this Christology Jesus Christ started out the same as you and I start out, with the same sort of givens, the same inherited capabilities, the same limitations of being in one finite body, in one point in history, in one location, in one particular culture. What he did with his givens somehow symbolizes the possibility for the achievement of fullness of potential in every human being. In this view the essence of the church (the body of Christ) becomes a group of human beings risking intimacy, sharing with one another the joys, the hurts, the whole range of what it's about to be human, and, thereby, attaining in its fullest moments the divine.

The model Jesus Christ established for intimacy was not that one gives oneself completely away, but that one makes sure somehow that everything one gives counts for the most. This requires a certain amount of planning and focusing of energy, a certain conscious restraint. Consider the way Jesus got to the major city where the most people were gathered at a most important festival with all the issues coming to a head, so that his death counted for the most. Intimacy involves not giving it all away and being left empty, but rather getting the cup filled as it is being emptied—receiving as well as getting.

B. Religio-Cultural Referents

The involvement of Christology with the process of human development at any stage as a universal factor puts us on the brink of a violation of the stated assumption in chapter 2. B.6. that this study avoids attempts to address the question of the existence and nature of God. Any implication of uniqueness on the part of Jesus Christ throws the discussion into the confusing and potentially destructive activity of affirming or denying "orthodox" concepts of the Trinity, the Godhead, and so forth because the non-Christian sources for a reconstruction of his life and personality are extremely slight.

As for use of the Christian sources, the late nineteenth and early twentieth century quest for the historical Jesus proved "too ambitious, too modern, and really impossible" when approached from the secular side. It was and is an essentially religious task.[4]

Thus, it would be dishonest to claim that the Christology of this stage and in this total study is anything more or less than my personal construction (reconstruction?) of an image or model of the nature and personality of Jesus Christ. That building process, as partly indicated in chapter 8.A., uses elements from church history, the Bible, theology, fiction, biography, psychology, and, probably most significantly, my own personal religious history to shape and reshape images of what and whom Jesus Christ was and is.

That image, at this writing, includes the following factors. Jesus the adult had the physical features of his Semitic forebears—dark hair, eyes, and skin. Probably small in height by current standards, he had calloused carpenter's hands, sun-darkened face, and sand-hardened feet. Of considerable intelligence, Jesus had sharpened his mental capability by serious study of Scripture and of human nature, and had accordingly become sensitive to the needs of individuals and his nation as a whole.

In late adolescence and beyond, there was in his consciousness a growing sense of some important purpose for his life which increasingly became tied to the expectations of the nation for a Messiah, a God-sent leader who would deliver Israel from her oppressors and bring in a golden age. The usual sexual longings, family loyalties, and vocational goals were sublimated to the rising sense of calling and the ever-sharpening understanding of his role, though not without considerable inner turmoil and resistance.

He gathered around him followers who shared freely their understandings of the role of the Messiah. In this give-and-take, Jesus' essential nature (especially his sensitivity to persons and their concerns) came into direct confrontation with the stereotype of militaristic messiah. Out of the tension produced by the confrontation came a synthesis in which Jesus became the Christ only he could become; a unique Christ only because each person is different in heredity, environment, development, and potential from every other person; a Christ wherein Jesus' potential was maximized; a Christ as every person has opportunity to become a Christ in a realized, fulfilled personhood.

Equally ambiguous and confusing are the religio-cultural referents of the word "intimacy." Dictionary and thesaurus definitions range from "illicit sexual commerce" and "fornication" through the milder "sexual relations" to "friendship," "closeness," "communion," "familiarity," and "that which pertains to the inmost being." Along with Erikson's definition cited earlier, the aspects or facets of intimacy delineated by the Clinebells in their book on marriage help further refine the meaning of the word as it is intended for us here.[5]

Intimacy, for the Clinebells and for me, involves risking greater openness, being emotionally present (available with minimal alienation), developing a high degree of caring, trusting based on commitment to fidelity and continuity, and respecting the need for periods of aloneness, of solitude. This intimacy is multidimensional and hopefully can occur sexually, emotionally, intellectually, aesthetically, creatively, recreationally, spiritually, and at the levels of work, commitment, and crises.[6]

C. Research Referents

Wayne Oates has isolated six religious ideas dominating the belief systems of certain mentally ill persons: the unpardonable sin, flesh versus spirit, the unforgiving legalist, the confusion of the God idea and the self, the end of the world, and the messianic idea. Two of these ideas are especially pertinent in the discussion of Christology gone pathological and observed in the clinical situation: the confusion of the God idea and the self and the messianic idea.[7]

In the person confusing himself with or claiming the identity of God, Jesus Christ, the Holy Spirit, or the Virgin Mary, Oates found three common threads: a desire to be perfect, a shattered self-concept, and a surly, fault-finding, suspicious attitude. Similarly, in individuals believing themselves to be in some sort of messianic identity, Oates found two common factors: a compulsive sense of necessity to carry out a specific task and an experiencing of life itself as basically meaningless.[8]

A fascinating blend of the two ideas is found in the poignant case of Elbert Jones, a fifty-seven-year-old, four-times-married, merchant seaman, the father of two children, seen by me on his second admission to a large state mental hospital.

He grew up in a home not formally linked to any institutional church. His father had been removed from good standing in a Baptist church for dancing. He described his mother simply as a "good woman." Two years before this hospitalization she had died of cancer in his home. Elbert had joined a Baptist church at age fourteen, but never felt really comfortable in that relationship.

He had met and courted his current wife while in a Mexican port. They never got along; she wanted security, insurance, the things money can buy. He was interested in the beauty of nature. Furthermore, he had increasing difficulty holding a job.

His first hospitalization resulted from an incident in which he impulsively fondled the genitals of a four-year-old neighbor girl. A member of Elbert's church arranged for his case to be filed away in exchange for admission to the mental hospital. He stayed several weeks, and the case was never brought to trial.

Then two months before the present admission, he began to hear a voice on board ship saying at first only "Christ, Christ, Christ." Soon the voice was speaking to Elbert continuously, quoting verses of Scripture and saying that Elbert was to bring God's judgment to the world. The voice gave specific instructions:

1. Go to the UN and tell the representatives there that God wants all nations to become a single world community.

2. Go to Viet Nam and stop the war.

3. Instruct the treasuries of the world to recall all money, which is then to be given out from a central treasury equally to all the world's people at the rate of five hundred dollars per week.

4. Preach the message found in Psalm 91. (God is my refuge.)

Elbert got off the ship at the next port, bought two hundred and fifty dollars worth of clothes so that he would be presentable for his divine mission, and flew to his home city. There he had his twenty-year-old daughter (whose husband was at that time stationed in Viet Nam) drive him to a stationery store where he bought deluxe stationery complete with gold seals and rented a typewriter. Then he dictated a letter to his daughter in which he requested time on a particular Sunday morning at his church whereupon he would reveal his identity and unveil his plan for the world.

The contents of the letter soon got to the church member who arranged to stay his original case; the bond was dropped, the sheriff picked him up, and he found himself back in the mental hospital. There, in discussions with staff members, he further elaborated his new task. On a certain day all of man's laws were to be dissolved, especially with regard to marriage. At that point Elbert would be free to marry his daughter, and then the two could preside over the world as Adam and Eve once did as the world gradually regressed to its original garden of Eden-like state.

I saw the meaning of all this as relating in some way to the inability to integrate incestuous impulses toward the daughter with an extremely rigid expectation of what a Christian person is supposed to be and feel and do. Further, I felt Elbert's inability to function for long as a breadwinner reinforced already extremely strong feelings of worthlessness. The economics of his frantic reach for a grand identity and a grandiose mission became obvious. "I must be worthwhile if I'm Christ returned!" "Life must have meaning if I'm to save the world!"

After a course of electroshock therapy, I found him seriously reexamining his experience, to wit: "The voice said, 'Christ, Christ,' over and over, but it did not specifically say 'You are Christ' or anything like that. I would sure be a fool to claim to be something I'm not!" He then quickly moved toward a more healthy acceptance of himself as a human being and was later discharged from the hospital.

Social psychologist Milton Rokeach's fascination with belief systems and mind-sets has produced significant contributions. One of these is his book, *The Open and Closed Mind* (1960). Another, a study also resulting in a book, *The Three Christs of Ypsilanti* (1964), is important not only for its insights into the nature of identity and belief, but is also significant as a nearly classic research effort in the psychopathological use of Christology. It is the popularly written account of a carefully arranged and elaborately executed study of the interactions and interrelationships in a group composed of three mental patients whose primitive belief systems were that they, individually, were Jesus Christ.[9]

Sadly, the three Christs of Ypsilanti did not recover a sense of personal identity from the confrontations with each other and with the researchers. Two of them were older, chronic, mental patients and showed the fewest signs of change in ideation. The youngest of the three, Leon, less psychotic, more subtly adapted his belief system in the face of the confrontations.[10]

Fascinating is the way in which the investigators' own stereotype of Jesus Christ crept into the evaluative process as "the gentlest and tenderest of men." The extreme difficulty in the conduct of meaningful research relating to Christology remains real. The idiographic methodology remains the most realistic to me.[11]

D. Intimacy Illuminative Case

Hanley was a twenty-nine-year-old, single, Protestant minister four months into his second hospitalization in a large state hospital when I inherited him from the previous chaplain on the first day of my new job assignment. He was a rather handsome, blond, young man of average height and weight whose slump in posture reflected his feelings about himself.

The basic concern became clear to me at the outset of that first of some eighty interviews spread over eleven months. He took a chair in my office and immediately edged back into a corner, dramatically illustrating and communicating his fear of getting close, his inability to experience intimacy.

From the start Hanley demonstrated strong ambivalent feelings toward me that mirrored a similar ambivalence toward the most important person in his life, namely, his mother. For example, at the end of that first interview he expressed both anger at what he termed my pushiness and fear because of my planned absence from the hospital for a brief vacation.

Early in our relationship Hanley indirectly indicated his difficulty in passage through the earlier life stages. He described himself as a "Non-A," his term for worthlessness, and dramatized this attitude by being unable to get any closer to the chapel sanctuary on Sunday than the vestibule; he wrote one letter to his mother each week and hated doing it basically because he had learned that one must do certain works to earn love; he shared his feeling that his mother never wanted him and that he felt responsible not only for his own salvation, but also for the salvation of his mother and two younger brothers. As we looked together at the messianic quality of this ideation, Hanley laughed nervously and said, "I've often thought that I am Christ returned, that now I am approaching age thirty . . ." (My own anxious response was to also laugh and say, "That's crazy.")

In the third interview Hanley introduced the subject of his homosexual struggles. He said he had done some acting out in his early teens and then again after getting into therapy with a psychiatrist on an outpatient basis. This produced strong guilt feelings, and he believed the behavior was linked to his relationship to his mother (much later on he shared his fearsome fantasy that all vaginas have teeth). Significantly, he stated the impossibility of integrating his sexual impulses with his idealized self-image as a "nice, religious guy."

Within the developmental psychology of religion framework, Hanley's distorted view of the nature of man was reinforced by his symbiotic relationship with his mother and by a religious education both stereotypic and unrealistic, to wit, "Good Christian men are never sexually attracted to other men (and especially never sexually attracted to their mothers)!"

Gradually our relationship warmed up, but on those occasions when I expressed my tender feelings for Hanley directly and verbally, he reacted with fright and wonder about why I would take such a risk. In later discussions of Hanley's homosexual bent, he saw it as helping him to avoid any lasting relationship or ongoing responsibility to another human being. At one point when I asked him who he might like to marry, he bluntly responded, "I guess I would like to marry my mother."

Another complication with Hanley involved a cultural-religious lesson he had learned exceedingly well, "Good Christian men should never get angry, especially without good reason, and doubly especially just because someone leaves said good Christian man by dying." Imagine Hanley's bind when his father, lying on his deathbed, said to Hanley, "Take care of your mother if anything happens to me."

Through my attempts to involve him in specific tasks in chapel services, which he consistently refused, we faced some factors involved in his entering the ministry. He concluded:

1. His calling was a life-and-death matter in that he needed to succeed as a minister to prove his identity as a man.

2. He had no outside interests and releases for his energies, no recreation, no hobbies, no intimacy with persons outside of his parish.

3. He could not see himself in any other meaningful work.

Over the months I almost had to literally push him toward contact and then involvement with a vocational rehabilitation program in which he later began to function as a teaching assistant in a hospital math class, thereby beginning to ease up a bit on (3) above.

Pressure to participate in ward activities, sports, dances and the like, plus the introduction of a warm, middle-aged female cotherapist into the process did combine to move him gradually toward the point of more relaxed functioning, more freedom to fantasize heterosexual pleasures, more willingness to risk himself in reaching out, in reducing the distance between himself and his fellow human beings.

Hanley left the hospital somewhat improved, somewhat less isolated.

E. Implications for Religious Education

The christological debate continues today. There are those within and outside the institutional churches who find themselves at the (left?) end of the christological spectrum which denies the divinity of Christ. These so-called liberals, for whatever reasons, find untenable and unfair the idea that one human being among all the human beings who ever lived or ever will live could, would, and should singularly enjoy the status of being a part of the Godhead and of being the only begotten Son of God.

At the other (right?) end of the christological spectrum are those, also both within and outside the structural church, who deny the humanity of Christ, if not openly, surely at the level of feeling and behavior. These so-called conservatives, again for varying reasons, find uncomfortable and unacceptable the idea that God's only begotten Son, Jesus Christ, could, would, and should have truly human feelings of rage, lust, envy, fear and the like to begin with, much less truly difficult experiences of managing and channeling those feelings in real-life situations.

Roughly analogous to the christological spectrum is an intimacy-isolation spectrum looming fairly visible in the life of the churches and denominations, and, less obviously, perhaps existing for individual persons as well. At one (left?) end are the groups (persons?) who seek total interrelationship with other groups (persons?; e.g., Bahá'í?) and thereby become totally syncretistic and watered down, absorbing into one bland identification the identities of the constituents (the organization man?).

On the opposite (right?) end of the intimacy-isolation spectrum are those churches and sects (persons?) who see themselves (holiness groups?) for whatever dynamic reasons, as totally self-sufficient, independent, even superior to other similar groups (persons?) and thereby seek a grand, self-perpetuating, noncritical, lonely course (hermits, researchers?).

Religious educators must help people learn the vivid dangers at either end of the theological, denominational, and personal spectra if in fact they are to continue to have any audience at all. My current stereotype of Jesus Christ is that of one person who, having weathered the developmental crises of trust-god, autonomy-good, initiative-redemption, industry-works, and identity-man in an extremely positive way, sought intimacy and, thereby, personal fulfillment, by striving for a middle ground interdependence with God and mankind which repudiates both total dependence and total independence. This, to me, is the model of Jesus Christ to be taught and emulated.

9

Generativity and Creation

A. The Specific Hypothesis Elaborated

Stage seven in Erikson's scheme is the one in which he says the psychosocial crisis concerns generativity versus self-absorption or stagnation. By generativity Erikson means that which is involved in establishing and guiding the next generation of humanity.

The theological issue in focus for people in this stage, which takes place in middle adulthood, is creation at the levels of experience and accomplishment. In the beginning God created the heavens and the earth. Similarly, in middle adulthood humanity creates and nurtures the next generation. This is when one attains maximum productivity, when one bumps into the limits of achievement, when one rises to his "level of incompetence," when one falls prey to the "If not now, when?" syndrome. Because this is the time when, among other things, one faces giving up some of the idealism of younger days. Not giving up ideals. Rather, coming to grips with the reality of reduced alternatives in life.

The farther along one gets in the educational process, the more specialized one gets, the fewer jobs are open, and the more committed one is with dollars first to a mate and then to children. When the dollars come in one is not quite as free to choose how to spend them as in an earlier stage. This involves a diminishing of hope. Some of the childhood and adolescent fancies and fantasies must die at this stage. One discovers that one is not really going to make it totally at whatever one wanted. One will likely not become president of the United States. For the business oriented, one will not likely make corporate president; for the artist, one will not be the greatest; for the athlete, one will not set all the world's records.

Here human beings are in the fullness of time in the sense of their being creative individuals and making use of the creativity they have—being engaged in the creation of life, literally, having children, raising a family; being engaged in the creation of meaningful products and services for the society at large in vocation; hopefully, being engaged in the creation of a purposeful life. Middle adults must take over the reins of leadership in the institutions of society, the government, the educational system, the transportation system, the economic system, the church.

It is a time when the individual discovers that he or she is beginning to slow down a bit physically. It is a time of the acceptance of authority, both one's own and others'; or if there isn't some kind of peace made with authority, one's own and others', there occurs then the pitiful phenomenon of the aging hippie.

Security needs somehow become more conscious. In one's experience, being reminded on every side of finitude, one's own death makes one unconsciously and consciously strive harder to defend against that inevitable end by surrounding oneself with cushions of one kind or another—creature comforts, insurance policies, a savings account. One finds a certain security and comfort in routine and familiar tasks, corridors, faces.

The psychosocial modality that Erikson cites at this point is to make be and to take care of. There is a resurgence of the latency issues of industry and works because work is tied very closely with this creative process. How does one avoid dying on the vine? How does one avoid getting so caught up with these comfort and security needs that one gets into a rut, that one literally begins to die, to get so caught up in self needs, as Erikson calls it self-absorption, that one is little more than a selfish child?

It is at this point there is often a search for renewal. In some of the expressions of the institutional church in days gone by and even in some churches now the word "revival" is an expression of this attempt to avoid the rut, to find renewal. We see it reflected in the Christian year in the season of Easter, the celebration of the resurrection of Christ even as around us we see the earth coming to life, turning green, blossoming forth.

Some people seem to seek to overcome stagnation by just picking up and moving. That accounts for some of the mobility in our society in which one out of every five families moves every year. At least a part of that movement is an expression of the need to crawl out of the rut, to provide a totally new structure so that one must be stimulated and turned on to the new environment. This is a time when again the leisure question comes up. Does one have an avocation to balance one's vocation? Does one have activities that one likes to do, places that one likes to be, things that one likes to see, simply for enjoyment and to replenish the energy expended in creative work? Does one have ways of getting one's cup refilled after it has been poured out in the creation process and in the operation of one's life, one's family, the program, the job, and so on? If most of the answers are yes, one has managed to be somehow creative. If most of the answers are no, one is in danger of stagnation and individual destruction.

B. Religio-Cultural Referents

The dictionary is, among other things, a rich reservoir of meanings brought to words by a particular culture. A consideration of dictionary meanings of the verb "create" provides several cultural referents: to bring into being; to cause to exist; to invest with a new form, office, or character; to constitute; to produce, form, or bring to pass by influence over others; to produce as a work of thought or imagination, as a work of art. The noun "creation" is seen as the creative act as well as something which has been created.

Religiously speaking, most civilizations and cultures have their own cosmologies, their own explanations of the origins of the world. Even within the Bible itself some scholars claim two distinct creation accounts with two authors distinctly different in style, word usage, and point of view.

The J story of creation (Gen. 2:4b–3:24) is a movingly ingenuous tale, profound in the issues it plumbs. Here the far-reaching questions about human origin and destiny are clothed in a form intelligible to the simplest mind, yet tantalizing to the wisest. The viewpoint of the tale is that of a Palestinian peasant, for Adam is none other than the tiller of the soil.

Again,

> The Priestly story of creation, although written much later than the Yahwist's story of the beginnings, has been introduced as a grand exordium to the Pentateuch. In the tremendous scope and pristine beauty of the account, the symmetry and magnitude of the creative acts, the editors saw a fitting way to introduce the wonderful works of Israel's God.[1]

Gottwald sees the accommodation of an originally untimed story about the obligation of Sabbath worship to the conception of a six-day divine workweek as both naïve and profound. I agree that the stipulation conferring on mankind the privilege of repetition of the divine rhythm of work and rest affirms mankind's participation with God in the sequence of activity and passivity, of creation and contemplation.[2]

Each of the religio-cultural factors introduced in the discussion of industry and works in chapter 6.B. earlier is brought to bear once again at the point of the "productive" years of middle adulthood. The lessons learned or unlearned, the individual's response to his particular set of religio-cultural pressures during the latency years will be revived, relived, and, hopefully, resolved in the effort to "generate," to "create."

Viennese psychiatrist Viktor E. Frankl, as a Jew, was subjected by the Nazis in World War II to unbelievably humiliating deprivations of freedom and dignity. As he struggled to maintain his sanity under these extremely depersonalizing conditions, he was forced to reexamine all his assumptions about human beings and their values. Out of his death-camp experiences, Frankl developed a philosophy of life and system of psychotherapy which have a special bearing on the issues of middle adulthood. Frankl holds that the discovery of meaning in life has a direct relationship, not with the conscious pursuit of happiness for its own sake, but rather with the discovery of a concrete life task relative to one's own unique singularity. As one masters these concrete tasks with which an occupation and family life present him, he becomes greater than the great man whose sphere of influence may be national or international in scope, yet whose decisions are without scruple and evil in consequence. This process Frankl describes as the realization of creative values.[3]

Probably the most obvious religio-cultural referent for Western civilization is the charge given by God to his newly created adults. "God blessed them, saying to them, 'Be fruitful, multiply, fill the earth and conquer it. Be masters of the fish of the sea, the birds of heaven and all living animals on the earth' " (Gen. 1:28).

C. Research Referents

James G. Emerson, Jr., writing in *Pastoral Psychology* some years ago, hypothesized four crisis stages within adulthood: three years out, the summit, retirement, and death. The first two possibilities are relevant to our discussion of middle adulthood's generativity, its creation, or stagnation. The second two are pertinent for the final stage in Erikson's scheme. Emerson admits his hypothesis is only that, but he does make use of clinical illustration to develop the hypothesis.[4]

He holds that the three-years-out crisis occurs somewhere between three to five years after a young adult has left the nurturing structure, or in the case of a professional, it may hit shortly after the last year of training. This crisis is characterized by not being able any longer to rely on the support and protection of either family or school. Characteristics, according to Emerson, include feelings of falling to pieces, dreams of being at sea or of falling, and ideas of being in the wrong work.

With particular respect to the ministry, Emerson's thesis regarding the three-years-out crisis gels some support from C. George Fitzgerald. Writing in *The Journal of Pastoral Care* Fitzgerald uses his own vocational history as a Presbyterian minister to point up what he sees as a moratorium or trial period of up to six or more years in which the minister is given limited responsibility, both in terms of parish assignment and denominational posts.[5]

Within recent years the mental health of doctors, lawyers, clergy, and other professionals has come under close scrutiny by researchers and popular writers. Some significant surveys of ministers in particular have been conducted. For example, the 1965 General Assembly of the Presbyterian Church in the U.S. initiated a study by psychiatrist Robert D. Phillips and seminary professor Thomas H. McDill entitled "The Mental Health of Presbyterian Ministers and Their

Families" in which 2,091 ministers and 1,899 ministers' wives responded to a questionnaire. Results, though admittedly inconclusive, pointed to societal pressures, suburban living patterns, and the decreasing prestige of the ministerial role as contributing to emotional problems of ministers.[6] Edgar W. Mills and other researchers continue to probe for data on the emotional and vocational stresses of ministers.

Emerson characterizes his second stage of adulthood, the summit, as requiring an increasing capacity for aloneness in the sense that the president of the United States can be said to have the loneliest job in the world. Not limited to the U.S. presidency, this aloneness is directly proportional to the size of the executive function exercised by the middle adult, to wit, "The buck stops here." In the summit imagery Emerson finds an advantage: From the top one can see clearly both sides. One can look back with satisfaction and forward with anticipation, ideally speaking.[7]

D. Generativity Illuminative Case

Jack is a thirty-eight-year-old minister in his third year as chaplain and director of pastoral care services at a large midwestern, state university teaching-hospital and an adjacent mental health center. His primary reason for seeking his present position related to his need to create. He had been working under extremely secure conditions in a setting familiar and pleasant for him: a large, southern, state hospital where he had trained for two years, had been invited to remain as a permanent staff chaplain in a substantial state merit system pay grade, and had been promoted to assistant chief chaplain status in order to specialize in an area of great interest to him—research.

Yet a strange restlessness plagued him. He became increasingly aware of the facts that the chaplaincy program had been developed by others, that despite the good features of his position he was one of many in a large department, that he yearned to develop his own program, to do his own thing.

When he learned of the opening in the Midwest and discovered that no one had ever held such a position there, he actively sought and was appointed to the new job. He is now literally bringing into being out of nothingness a sophisticated program of pastoral care for patients and their families and a program of clinical pastoral education for seminarians and clergy. This demanding task he finds rewarding beyond its material benefits in that it meets his strong need to be generative, productive, creative. He is doing his own thing and loving it.

Jack has discovered, furthermore, that his drive toward creation is multidimensional, that it has within the last few years permeated every aspect of his experience. For example, after six years of marriage Jack and his wife had no children, despite many medical consultations and one extensive surgical procedure. Jack, then age thirty, and his wife felt strongly enough the desire for creation in the sense of bringing children into the family that they initiated adoption proceedings. After a strangely appropriate waiting period of nine months, they brought home their new child, a laughing, three-month-old, baby boy.

Within two years the creative urge surfaced again in their request for a second child. After a year's wait this time, they, along with their son, made the exciting trip to meet the fourth member of the family, a tiny, six-week-old, red-haired, red-faced, baby girl.

On another level, Jack found himself drawn toward writing as a creative expression of his personality. True enough, a part of his desire to write involved the ego satisfaction of getting published and seeing his name in print; a part was tied to his need for immortality via being "in the literature." Yet it was more. Again, and perhaps primarily, it was to feel the pleasure of bringing into being something out of nothing, of placing words on the page in a way they had never been placed before, of creativity, of making a contribution.

Several minor journal articles were published. He even submitted two poems to a local poetry magazine. Interestingly, the autobiographical poem was rejected while the descriptive poem was accepted. Here is the autobiographical one.

MIDWAY

Midway is my Middle Name
My little game
My life style
My strength
My sin
My neurosis.

Midway is where I live.
On the map it's
    Midway
    between
Alphalpha and Omegalopolis.

Generativity and Creation

Not too cold
Not too hot
Is what I've got. . . .

The missing link
    between
The Great Depression
    and
Nineteen Eighty Four
    between
East and West
North and South
The Poor House
    and
    Many Mansions
Wisdom and Folly
Module and Trolley
Fallout and Volley
Fibber McGee
    and
        Zooey.

E. Implications for Religious Education

Church programs for leadership training and development are directly involved in helping persons in the crisis of middle adulthood. These already existing efforts plus those bringing the tenets of a particular faith to bear on the developmental tasks of the middle years in a way enhancing creativity would likely find a positive response among the congregations. Such tasks include achieving adult civic and social responsibility, establishing and maintaining an adequate economic standard of living, assisting teen-aged children in becoming responsible and happy adults, developing adult, leisure-time activities, relating oneself to one's spouse as a person, accepting and adjusting to the physiological changes of middle age, and adjusting to aging parents.[8]

Another, an existential dimension can be added and focused upon through Clinebell's ninth test for mentally healthy religion: "Does a particular form of religious thought and practice give its adherents a 'frame of orientation and object of devotion' that is adequate in handling existential anxiety constructively?" Clinebell maintains, and I agree, that existential anxiety is most adequately coped with by a vital religious life which includes a meaningful philosophy of life, a challenging object of devotion, a sense of transcendence above the earthboundness of life, and a deep experience of trust in God and relatedness to the universe.[9]

10

Integrity and Eschatology

A. The Specific Hypothesis Elaborated

Erikson's eighth and final developmental stage poses a central issue: whether or not an individual can get in touch with a certain integrity about the particular life he or she has lived. If so, it is because one can look back and see that life had meaning, purpose, fulfillment. If not, one despairs, one views death with a desperate fear born of the fact that death denies the opportunity to do it all over again differently. Erikson sees the psychosocial modalities at this stage as to be through having been and to face not being.

Thus, the theological issue in the final life-cycle crisis becomes eschatology, the doctrine of last things. Eschatology is a theological technical term taken from the Greek word for last and encompasses the whole body of biblical materials and religious tradition relating to the end of time, the last days of creation, and what it means for individuals. In this study the focus is not on universal, but rather personal, eschatological concerns.

Formal religion at its best offers support to persons in passage through this stage by affirming the dignity of individual human life, by offering forgiveness for earlier errors and sins, by even helping one come full circle in a return to a lifting up of basic trust, of gods, of God. Erikson cites Noah Webster at this point in his definition of trust as assured reliance on another's integrity.

There is a return to first things on other levels at this time of concern with last things: a gradual relinquishing of authority and power; a decreasing of actual physical motor ability and the increasing of dependency upon others; a shrinking of one's world, perhaps culminating in a sick room or hospital bed.

In our Western civilization two factors make last things more difficult—the phenomenon of formal retirement at a particular age, usually sixty-five, and deeply engrained denial of death. With retirement, lessons learned too well at the works and creation stages may bring on, at least unconsciously, the self-estimate, "I cannot produce anymore; therefore, I am not worth anything anymore." Such an awesome assessment is made more painful by the discovery—through illnesses, the death of friends, associates, and perhaps even a mate—that after all of our denial of death, we still face death.

The Viennese psychiatrist, Viktor Frankl, was forced by circumstances of his apprehension by the Nazis in Europe as a Jew to face prematurely some sort of resolution of his integrity-despair personal eschatology. Out of that struggle, out of the horror of being stripped of his rights, his property, his family, and his dignity as a human being, Frankl came to the realization that there is one element which remains inviolable—the right to choose one's attitude toward a given situation. By great exercise of personal will he decided to live, to find meaning in his existence, to maintain a certain attitudinal integrity, thereby providing an exceptionally clear example of the avoidance of total despair in a despair-filled situation: being a Jewish prisoner in a Nazi death camp. Forcibly "retired" from his job as a practicing psychiatrist, he found meaning in day-to-day and unexpected situations related both to his work as a slave laborer and to his "off-duty" relationships to his fellow prisoners.[1]

Another psychiatrist, Elizabeth Kübler-Ross, has shed some light upon the feelings of persons facing their own death. She and her students interviewed five hundred dying patients and found, among other things, that for the most part people do not fear death per se, but, more particularly, fear violent death. She also identified several stages through which individuals pass in coming to grips with their own death, the last of which is a certain peaceful acceptance. Those who achieved this final acceptance often had experienced a "transfer of hope," a shifting of the wish for personal survival to the wish for some accomplishment by another.[2] For example, the dying patient might begin to say, "I hope the children can complete college."

These are the persons who have enough of a sense of integrity about their lives to be able to look beyond their own fates to the hopes of others. These are the ones who are able to sense that their own particular individual life cycle is related to the corporate life cycle of mankind. Erikson speaks of this phenomenon as the ability for *followership*, to be able to be a part of the larger cause, a greater movement than oneself.

Either life is worth living or it isn't. If life is worth it, one finds a sense of calm, peaceful integrity and a return to basic trust. If not, the bitter, angry, fearful, pathetic, last things are only too clear to see.

B. Religio-Cultural Referents

For I have reflected on all this and come to understand that the virtuous and the wise with all they do are in the hand of God. Man does not know what love is, or hate, and both of these in his eyes are vanity. Just as one fate comes to all, to virtuous as to wicked, to clean and unclean, to him who sacrifices and him who does not sacrifice, so it is with the good man and the sinner, with him who takes an oath and him who shrinks from it. This is the evil that inheres in all that is done under the sun: that one fate comes to all; further, that the hearts of men should be full of malice; that they should practise such extravagances towards the living in their lifetime, and the dead thereafter. For anyone who is linked with all that live still has some hope, a live dog being better than a dead lion. The living know at least that they will die, the dead know nothing; no more reward for them, their memory has passed out of mind. Their loves, their hates, their jealousies, these all have perished, nor will they ever again take part in whatever is done under the sun (Eccles. 9:1–6).

On the other hand,

I will tell you something that has been secret: that we are not all going to die, but we shall all be changed. This will be instantaneous, in the twinkling of an eye, when the last trumpet sounds. It will sound, and the dead will be raised, imperishable, and we shall be changed as well, because our

120

present perishable nature must put on imperishability and
this mortal nature must put on immortality. When this
perishable nature has put on imperishability, and when
this mortal nature has put on immortality, then the words
of scripture will come true: . . . "Death, where is your victory? Death, where is your sting?" Now the sting of death is
sin, and sin gets its power from the Law. So let us thank
God for giving us the victory through our Lord Jesus Christ
(I Cor. 15:51–57).

Aging, currently defined as "decline, involution, or
loss of functional capacity of the individual as a whole
or in part as it may affect total functioning,"
(whichever extreme one anticipates for life beyond the
grave), is, at least partly, preparation to meet death.[3]

In the opening sentence of his book, Milton McC.
Gatch succinctly sums up the twentieth century
religio-cultural referents on death. "It is one of the
ironies of our century that we have experienced death
by violence of sorts and on a scale heretofore unknown
but that men in this century have not been able to
discuss or to consider deeply the meaning of death."[4]

In the face of the inability to deal with death meaningfully, denial has become the Western religio-
cultural defense mechanism. Christian ministers continue to ply the primarily Greek, not biblical, theme of
the immortality of the soul. Funeral directors continue
to disguise the fact of death with slumber rooms, mat-
tressed caskets, cosmetics, and fake grass. Hospital
census reports refer to individuals' deaths with the
word "expired." Western culture increasingly treats
mourning as "morbid self-indulgence," giving "social
admiration to the bereaved who hide their grief so fully
that no one would guess anything had happened."[5]

Gatch, finding twentieth century theologians' professional stake in or commitment to a metaphysical point of view something of an encumbrance, looks to three distinct, forthright treatments of death in the modern novel as significant. First, in Thomas Mann's *Death in Venice*, Gatch sees "a picture of life and death which stresses the isolation of modern man and employs the mode of immortality to depict that isolation as a spiritual, non-historical struggle for salvation by means of discovery of the ideal form of truth and beauty."[6]

Second, in *The Death of Ivan Ilyich* (Leo Tolstoy), Gatch finds no hint of an afterlife, only existence in this world. But there is what some might consider a curious form of salvation for Ilyich when, at the close of his life, he agonizingly acknowledges its meaningless banality, finds his fear of death dissipated, and commits one last merciful act.[7]

Third, in Albert Camus' *The Plague*, an allegory about World War II in which the reactions of a number of residents of Oran, Algeria, to being caught in a bubonic plague epidemic are described, Gatch finds a linkup of at least one twentieth century stance toward death with that of the earliest Christians. "One must respond to the needs of others in the face of a crisis which no one can control." This "rediscovery of the community of man" is all the more powerful for its lack of heroics and for its emphasis upon the ordinary and seemingly insignificant. The linkup is not complete, however. Although Camus is able to relate man's struggle to exist from day to day with a larger historical struggle, and thereby to "endow the struggle with a note of urgency" (as did the early Christians), he is not able to tie together past events and the present within an all-encompassing purpose. "Life is purposive in that the community of men finds ways to cope with the absurd; but life is isolated in that there is no continuum within which the community of men can formulate the universal or historical significance of their experience in the face of death."[8]

Gatch concludes,

> The modern novels discussed above suggest that there have been ways to talk about death in the modern period which have been more direct and more concerned with the mundane than many philosophical discussions. Even Mann's approach by way of the life of the soul displays a certain concern for everyday events as reflecting a spiritual reality. Tolstoy and Camus are able, because of their more direct concern with ordinary reality for its own sake and with the day-to-day events in the lives of their characters, to achieve a far greater impression of the relationship of man's death to his living. But all three novels demonstrate in varying degrees the isolation of modern man. He exists as a center of subjectivity observing and participating in events which are not part of a purposive continuum but are themselves isolated and self-contained. At the same time as the modern novel may show us ways to talk about death, then, it presents in a graphic and classical way the chief problem of man in the modern world: the fact that the individual is trapped by self and subjectivity.[9]

C. Research Referents

The third and fourth substages of adulthood hypothesized by Emerson, retirement and death, are relevant here. In the realm of retirement issues there is an increasing interest and a burgeoning literature. Among those writing in the area of retirement and its problems for meaningful pastoral care are J. Paul Brown, Clarence Butler, and J. E. Runions. However, only one research project is listed in *Pastoral Care and Counseling Abstracts* in geriatrics in 1972.[10]

A one-hundred-item Goal Questionnaire, which paired seventeen life goals most frequently chosen by normal subjects twenty to thirty-three years of age with eighteen life goals most frequently chosen by normal subjects over sixty years of age, was given to ninety subjects divided into two age groups, one middle-aged (forty to fifty-four) and one older (fifty-five and over), across cultural-economic lines.

The study's main hypothesis, that depressed subjects would choose a greater number of younger goals than a similar group of normal subjects, was confirmed at a high level of confidence. A second hypothesis, that the middle-aged group would choose more younger goals than the older group was also supported at a high confidence level. Other hypotheses (e.g., whether failure to achieve life goals was a factor in depressed persons' tendency to cling to younger goals) were not supported by the data.[11]

As for research in the area of death and dying, there has been a flood of material in recent years. In an interesting summary of the current scene, J. William Worden, writing a guest editorial, "On Researching Death," for *Pastoral Psychology,* states his opinion that thanatology, the study of death, has overcome societal taboos to the extent that it has now almost become a subspecialty of psychology, psychiatry, nursing, and the social sciences.[12] The discipline of pastoral care and counseling could be added to the list when one considers that two recent issues of the now defunct *Pastoral Psychology* (November, 1971 and June, 1972) plus the June, 1972, *Journal of Pastoral Care* all plied the theme of death and dying and its pastoral implications.

Worthy of note are Worden's observations about future directions for death and dying research efforts. He elaborates five needs if such research is to be worthy of the name: the need for systematic observation (Did each of Dr. Kübler-Ross' five hundred patients pass through the same five stages?); the need to operationalize concepts (Do we agree on what we mean when we say a patient is denying?); the need for integrated theory (Can psychologists, sociologists, anthropologists, and theologians share from their particular areas of expertise their knowledge?); the need for multivariate data analysis (So far most of the data is descriptive and univariate.); and the need for interdisciplinary research teams (Each observer can see with his trained eye that which others, by virtue of different professional orientations, often do not see.).[13]

D. Integrity Illuminative Case

Theresa is a solidly built, white-haired, rosy-cheeked, fifty-eight-year-old Roman Catholic sister. She was born and raised with her three brothers by her mother and dry-goods-store-owner father. Her memories of life with her family are almost idyllic: family expeditions in the mountains of their native

Wyoming on weekends; parents "in love until the day my father died nine years ago"; enjoyment of her place as her father's favorite.

But there were subtle controls. Theresa now identifies her basic family role back then as mediator for her brothers and companion for her mother, even when she didn't want to be those things. And Father's word was law. A red thread running throughout her life concerns her attempts to maintain integrity while submitting to a demanding father-god-church. Father decreed that she would enter public high school. Regarding college, "There was never any real question of any other school." Her wish to become a doctor was blocked "since, at that time, we had no women doctors."

Academia has been a great part of her life. From a Catholic grade school, two years in a girls' academy, two years of public high school, a Catholic college, a Catholic university, through some fifteen full- and part-time experiences in various graduate schools, she has achieved various honors for her scholarship.

Obviously, the church has affected her life profoundly. From the solid, Catholic, religious base of her family she moved rather easily to the novitiate half-way through college and then to teacher of math and chemistry at the high school and college levels; she served also as principal of a large high school and as superior for her order's nearby house. Always deeply identified with the church, Theresa seemed to turn there for help in controlling her strong urges to be free. She willingly submitted to the then severe disciplines of the novitiate, almost as if she hoped the strong external controls would snuff out the rebel, the free spirit in her. Happily, it didn't work out that way. She found herself unable to accept blindly and unthinkingly that which others thought she should. This came more into focus with increasing responsibility. While serving as a superior, "I felt very caught between my role as representative of authority and my own ideas which were somewhat more liberal."

She discovered an opportunity to train as a basic clinical pastoral education student almost by accident while doing volunteer work with alcohol and drug addiction patients during a vocational rehabilitation master's program, an endeavor she entered to equip herself to help drug addicts and their families, sisters forced to retire and faced with years of idle time, and her own boredom with the classroom, her own personal "vocational rehabilitation." She was seeking a way to help older sisters and herself avoid "deterioration" via what she calls a "second career."

Assigned to a hospital's physical medicine and rehabilitation area plus an adult psychiatric ward as a clinical pastoral education student, she approached patients with a strong need to "do" "things" for them, to emphasize the positive, to cheer up. She was too authoritative, too directive. Gradually, through feedback from her peer group and the vocational rehabilitation people, she considered other alternatives, cultivated her ability to listen, dulled her autonomic reflex to defend the faith at the slightest hint of a challenge, and began to consider the theological significance and power of simply being with, even when you don't know just what to do or say. She worked mostly with females, establishing several significant helping relationships, and tended to go beyond the usual limits of involvement emotionally and practically (e.g., asking patients out for dinner). With staff she gained respect, partly through her contributions about patients (she got the shock of a lifetime when a psychiatrist called her "Protestant" during one discussion) and partly through her aggressive concern. (She asked one rather cool nurse if there was anything wrong.) She even won over an abrupt, gruff, old psychiatrist.

Theresa experimented a few times during the training with not wearing her veil to see if persons would relate to her differently. The experiment ended when she became too uncomfortable with the task of taking special care of her hair.

Her refusal to despair, her desire to find new challenge, her need to make "last things" in her lifetime count for as much as her earlier achievements, all these factors combined to make her clinical pastoral education experience extremely meaningful for her supervisor as well as for herself.

A measure of her integrity and the impact of this new training experience is the fact that she arranged, after completion of the program, to go to a large Catholic hospital in another city and set up a similar educational situation, thus accomplishing her earlier stated goal of finding a purposeful second career.

E. Implications for Religious Education

Havighurst lists as the developmental tasks of later maturity adjusting to decreasing physical strength and health, adjusting to retirement and reduced income, adjusting to death of spouse, establishing an explicit affiliation with one's age group, meeting social and civic obligations, and establishing satisfactory physical living arrangements. There can be little chance for significant ministry to persons in the crisis of integrity-eschatology without sensitivity to and structures for coming to grips with these developmental issues.[14]

Beyond the immediate needs of the elderly, there is the consideration of religious education about death and dying during the entire life cycle of the membership. Along with the usual exposure of children to loss by death of pets, grandparents, and the like, and the adjunctive teaching opportunities inherent in such situations, there is the possibility of structured sessions in death education for older church groups.

The best resource for practical death education in the church setting which I have found is an extensive and detailed essay plus expansive bibliography by Robert E. Neale, Associate Professor, Program in Psychiatry and Religion, Union Theological Seminary (N.Y.), in which he carefully outlines the content and procedure for each of six sessions. The subjects for the six sessions are denial, fear, grief, parts I and II, belief, and martyrdom.[15]

11

Conclusion

We have just completed a theological trip through the psychosocially segmented human life cycle from birth to death on the trail blazed by Erik Erikson. As the doctrinal markers were placed along the way, hopefully the pathway becomes more clearly visible to busy pastors, religious education directors, Sunday school teachers, and concerned lay persons who seek to understand themselves more fully and to minister to others more sensitively.

Whether or not insights have been shared in a style acceptable to those other than my fellow clinicians, whether or not this developmental psychology of religion (or should it have been called a developmental theology?) moves toward a rapprochement of theological and psychological principles, of course, must be decided by the reader.

Whatever the decision, it should be noted that the very exercise of writing my way through the eight stages has stirred more profound questions. Does the scheme have meaning for more than just the life cycle and theological development of an individual human being? Could there be such a developmental process in the religious consciousness and expressions of humankind at large? (The recapitulation theory, that the human race passes through the same stages of belief that the individual passes through, is well known to students of the history of religions.) If so, where are we in such a process at this historical moment?

In the chapter on initiative, sin, and redemption, I speculated that the coming together of God-is-dead theology and Freudian psychology at this point in history suggests that Western culture-religion is in its Oedipal stage. One variation of that, which I hope to explore in another writing project soon, is that the period of the beginnings of those world religions having personal founders (roughly the 1,200-year period from Mahavira to Muhammed and including Gautama, Lao-Tze, Confucius, Zoroaster, and Jesus) is more reasonably equatable with the initiative-sin-redemption stage, having been preceded by a trust-God stage (animism) and an autonomy–good-evil stage (the systematization of polytheism and the rise of national religions). Having already passed through an industry-works stage (the institutionalization of the personally founded religions) and most of an adolescent identity-man stage (the demythologizing of the institutionalized personal religions), could we be on the threshold of a humankind-coming-of-age-religiously, intimacy Christology stage of remythologizing the personal religions?

I think so.

Notes

Chapter 1

1. Adapted from Robert Coles, "The Measure of Man-1," *The New Yorker* (November 7, 1970), pp. 51-131.
2. Erik H. Erikson, *Childhood and Society*, 2nd rev. ed., paper (New York: W. W. Norton & Co., 1964).
3. Erikson, *Young Man Luther: A Study in Psychoanalysis and History* (New York: W. W. Norton & Co., 1958); *Gandhi's Truth* (New York: W. W. Norton & Co., 1969); *Insight and Responsibility* (New York: W. W. Norton & Co., 1964); *Identity: Youth and Crisis* (New York: W. W. Norton & Co., 1968); see especially "Identity and the Life Cycle: Selected Papers," *Psychological Issues*, vol. 1 (1959).
4. Adapted from Erikson, "Worksheet," *Psychological Issues*, vol. 1 (1959), p. 166; *Childhood and Society*, chapter 7.

Chapter 2

1. These stages of human development roughly corresponding to Erikson's eight ages of man.
2. "On the Religion of Psychology" (Paper presented to the Department of Religious Services, Central State Hospital, Milledgeville, Ga. in October, 1969, later published in the ACPE South Central Region Research Bulletin, 1st quarter, 1972).
3. Russell Olt, *An Approach to the Psychology of Religion* (Boston: Christopher Publishing House, 1956), chapter 2; Paul E. Johnson, *Psychology of Religion*, rev. ed. (Nashville: Abingdon Press,

[1959], p. 15; Robert H. Thouless, *An Introduction to the Psychology of Religion*, 3rd ed., paper (London: Cambridge University Press, 1972), p. 8; Wayne E. Oates, *The Religious Dimensions of Personality* (New York: Association Press, 1957), chapter 6; Johnson, *Psychology of Religion*, p. 5; Samuel Southard, "Can Research Be Religious?" address to Association of Mental Health Chaplains, May, 1969; Thouless, *Introduction to Psychology of Religion*, p. 8; Hideo Kishimoto, "An Operational Definition of Religion," *Numen*, vol. 8 (1961); Paul W. Pruyser, *A Dynamic Psychology of Religion* (New York: Harper & Row, 1968), p. 8.

4. Orlo Strunk, Jr., "Relationships of Psychology of Religion and Clinical Pastoral Education," *Pastoral Psychology* (October, 1971), p. 34.

5. G. Stephens Spinks, *Psychology and Religion* (Boston: Beacon Press, 1963), p. 6.

6. Adapted from Samuel Southard, "Research in Pastoral Care," notes, Columbia Theological Seminary, Decatur, Ga.

Chapter 3

1. C. F. D. Moule, "The New Testament God," *The Interpreter's Dictionary of the Bible*, 4 vols. (Nashville: Abingdon Press, 1962) vol. 2, p. 432.

2. Robert Young, *Young's Analytical Concordance to the Bible*, rev. ed. (Grand Rapids: Eerdmans Publishing Co., 1955), p. 333.

3. *The Portable World Bible*, paper (New York: The Viking Press, 1968). "The Mother of All Things," p. 542, and "The Eternal Tao," p. 547. See also Sigmund Freud, trans. James Strachey, *Totem and Taboo*, paper (New York: W. W. Norton & Co., 1952), p. 152.

4. M. O. Nelson and E. M. Jones, "An Application of the Q-Technique to the Study of Religious Concepts," *Psychological Reports*, no. 3 (1957), pp. 293–97.

5. Orlo Strunk, Jr., "Perceived Relationships Between Parental and Deity Concepts," *Psychological Newsletter*, no. 10 (1959), pp. 222–26.

6. L. J. Adkins in a September, 1963, personal communication to Bernard Spilka and cited in Spilka *et al.*, "The Concept of God: A Factor-Analytical Approach," *Review of Religious Research*, no. 6 (1964), pp. 28–36.

Notes

7. Antoine Vergote et al. "Concept of God and Parental Images," *Journal for the Scientific Study of Religion*, vol. 3 (Spring, 1969), pp. 79–87.
8. Earnest Harms, "The Development of Religious Experience in Children," *American Journal of Sociology*, vol. 50 (September, 1944), pp. 112–22.
9. John J. Gleason, Jr., "God Concept Drawings of Emotionally Disturbed and Normal Adolescents," manuscript (1969).
10. Frank Lake, *Clinical Theology* (London: Darton, Longman & Todd, 1966).
11. *Ibid.*, pp. 673, 679.
12. *Ibid.*, p. 684.
13. *Ibid.*, p. 685.
14. Carroll A. Wise, *The Meaning of Pastoral Care* (New York: Harper & Row, 1966), pp. 109, 107–18.
15. Howard J. Clinebell, Jr., *Mental Health Through Christian Community* (Nashville: Abingdon Press, 1965), p. 32.

Chapter 4

1. "Good" in Hebrew means that a person or a thing is in accordance with the acknowledged practical, moral, or religious standards. J. Hempel, *The Interpreter's Dictionary of the Bible*, vol. 2, pp. 440–47.
2. "Evil" both in Hebrew and Greek usage, has primarily a pragmatic and qualitative sense. As judged by its effect or its appearance, something is evil when it is worthless, corrupt, displeasing, ugly, sad, painful, or injurious. E. Dinkler, *The Interpreter's Dictionary*, pp. 182-83.
3. Edward Langton, *Essentials of Demonology* (London: Epworth Press, 1949), pp. 219–24, vii.
4. Mary Baker Eddy, quoted in Frank S. Mead, *Handbook of Denominations in the U. S.*, 5th ed. (Nashville: Abingdon Press, 1970), p. 70.
5. Marcus Aurelius, quoted in "Good and Evil," *Great Books of the Western World*, vol. 2, p. 610.
6. Frank Lake, *Clinical Theology*, pp. 949, 954, 1071–72.
7. Haim G. Ginott, *Between Parent and Child* (New York: Avon Books, 1969), pp. 167–68.
8. Howard J. Clinebell, Jr., *Mental Health*, p. 32.

Chapter 5

1. John B. Noss, *Man's Religions*, rev. ed. (New York: The Macmillan Co., 1956), p. 26.
2. Sigmund Freud, *Totem and Taboo*, p. 132.
3. *Ibid.*, p. 141.
4. *Ibid.*, p. 154.
5. Dietrich Bonhoeffer, *Letters and Papers from Prison*, paper (New York: The Macmillan Co., 1953), pp. 219–20.
6. Thomas J. J. Altizer, *The Gospel of Christian Atheism* (Philadelphia: The Westminster Press, 1966), p. 113.
7. Thomas W. Ogletree, *The Death of God Controversy*, paper (Nashville: Abingdon Press, 1966), p. 90.
8. Freud, *Totem and Taboo*, p. 154.
9. Freud, ed. James Strachey, trans. Joan Riviere, *The Ego and the Id* (New York: W. W. Norton & Co., 1961), p. 44.
10. Edward V. Stein, *Guilt: Theory and Therapy* (Philadelphia: The Westminster Press, 1968), pp. 58, 59.
11. Melanie Klein, *The Psychoanalysis of Children*, 3rd ed. (London: Hillary House Publishers, Ltd., 1969), pp. 180–97.
12. Erich Fromm, *Man For Himself* (New York: Fawcett World Library, 1968), p. 144.
13. Stein, *Guilt*, p. 47.
14. David P. Ansubel, *Ego Development and the Personality Disorders* (New York: Grune & Stratton, Inc., 1952), p. 8.
15. Ralph Metzner quoted in Stein, *Guilt*, p. 139.
16. Howard J. Clinebell, Jr., *Mental Health*, pp. 34–35.

Chapter 6

1. G. W. F. Hegel, quoted in "Labor," *Great Books of the Western World*, vol. 2, p. 921.
2. John Calvin, trans. Beveridge, *Institutes of the Christian Religion*, 2 vols. (Grand Rapids: Eerdmans Publishing Co., 1953); Williston Walker, *A History of the Christian Church* (New York: Charles Scribner's Sons, 1959), p. 351.
3. Max Weber, *The Protestant Ethic and the Spirit of Capitalism* (New York: Scribners, 1930).
4. Thomas Luckmann, *The Invisible Religion* (New York: The Macmillan Co., 1967), p. 22.

5. Morton B. King and Richard A. Hunt, "Measuring the Religious Variable: Replication," *Journal for the Scientific Study of Religion*, vol. 2 (September, 1972), pp. 240–51.
6. *Ibid.*, pp. 248–50.
7. The items were rated as follows, with K=knowledge, B=belief, F=feeling, and W=works oriented. Four items rated W and one rated F appeared twice, and are circled.

    I. Creedal Assent
        1. B
        2. B
        3. B
        4. B
        5. B
        6. B
        7. B

    II. Devotionalism
        1. W
        2. W
        3. W
        4. Ⓦ
        5. Ⓕ

    III. Congregational Involvement
      A. Church Attendance
        1. W
        2. W
        3. W
      B. Organizational Activity
        1. W
        2. W
        3. W
        4. W
        5. W
        6. W

C. Financial Support
1. W
2. W
3. W
4. W
5. W

IV. Religious Knowledge
1. K
2. K
3. K
4. K
5. K
6. K
7. K
8. K

V. Orientation to Religion
A. Growth and Striving
1. W
2. Ⓦ
3. Ⓦ
4. Ⓦ
5. W
6. Ⓦ
B. Extrinsic
1. W
2. W
3. W
4. W
5. W
6. W
7. W

VI. Salience
A. Behavior
1. W
2. W

138

3. W
4. W
5. Ⓦ
6. W
7. W
B. Cognition
   1. B
   2. Ⓦ
   3. W
   4. Ⓦ
   5. Ⓕ

8. Wayne E. Oates, *Confessions of A Workaholic* (Nashville: Abingdon Press, Apex ed., 1972), pp. 92–97.

Chapter 7

1. Erik H. Erikson, "Reflections on the Dissent of Contemporary Youth," *International Journal of Psycho-Analysis*, vol. 51, (1970), pp. 13–14.
2. Perry LeFevre, *Understandings of Man*, paper (Philadelphia: The Westminster Press, 1966).
3. Charles William Stewart, *Adolescent Religion* (Nashville: Abingdon Press, 1967), p. 28.
4. *Ibid.*, pp. 294, 295.
5. J. Conrad Glass, Jr., "Premarital Sexual Standards Among Church Youth Leaders: An Exploratory Study," *Journal for the Scientific Study of Religion*, vol. 11 (December, 1972), pp. 362–63.
6. *Ibid.*, pp. 363, 364.
7. John J. Gleason, Jr., "Lucy and Logotherapy: A Context, A Concept, and A Case," *Voices*, vol. 7 (Spring, 1971), pp. 57–62.
8. Howard J. Clinebell, Jr., *Mental Health*, pp. 39, 40.

Chapter 8

1. Erik H. Erikson, *Childhood and Society*, p. 263.
2. Williston Walker, *History of the Christian Church*, p. 139.

3. William Norman Pittenger, *The Word Incarnate* (New York: Harper & Brothers, 1959), p. 92.
4. For a discussion of those sources see F. C. Grant, *The Interpreter's Dictionary of the Bible*, vol. 2, p. 877.
5. Howard J. Clinebell, Jr., and Charlotte H. Clinebell, *The Intimate Marriage* (New York: Harper & Row, 1970), pp. 25–27.
6. *Ibid.*, pp. 28–32.
7. Wayne E. Oates, *Religious Factors in Mental Illness* (New York: Association Press, 1955), chapter 2.
8. *Ibid.*
9. A primitive belief in Rokeach's typology is in part one which is central in an individual's belief system, and, therefore, very resistant to change; Milton Rokeach, *The Three Christs of Ypsilanti* (New York: Alfred A. Knopf, 1964).
10. *Ibid.*, pp. 317–19.
11. *Ibid.*, p. 325. A good example of the use of the idiographic approach is found in A. E. Bayer, "The Man Who Died: A Narrative Account of the Dutch Fisherman, Lou, and His Group," *Review of Religious Research*, vol. 10 (Winter, 1969), pp. 81–88.

Chapter 9

1. Norman K. Gottwald, *A Light to the Nations* (New York: Harper & Brothers, 1959), pp. 224–25; pp. 455–63.
2. *Ibid.*, p. 456.
3. Viktor E. Frankl, *Man's Search for Meaning*, paper (New York: Simon & Schuster, 1970); Frankl, *The Doctor and the Soul* (New York: Random House, 1973), pp. 34–35.
4. James G. Emerson, Jr., "Crisis in Adult Life: A Hypothesis," *Pastoral Psychology*, vol. 17 (November, 1966), pp. 9–16.
5. C. George Fitzgerald, "Ordination Plus Six," *The Journal of Pastoral Care.* vol. 21 (March, 1967), pp. 15–23.
6. "The Mental Health of Presbyterian Ministers and Their Families," pamphlet, Board of Church Extension, Presbyterian Church, U.S., 341 Ponce de Leon, N.E., Atlanta, Ga. 30308.
7. Emerson, "Crisis in Adult Life," p. 14.
8. Robert J. Havighurst, *Human Development and Education* (New York: Longmans, Green and Co., 1953), pp. 169–276.
9. Howard J. Clinebell, *Mental Health*, pp. 46, 47.

Notes

Chapter 10

1. Viktor Frankl, *Man's Search for Meaning*, pp. 1–214.
2. Elizabeth Kübler-Ross, *On Death and Dying*, paper (New York: The Macmillan Co., 1970).
3. *Psychiatry and the Aged: An Introductory Approach*, Group for the Advancement of Psychiatry, report no. 59.
4. Milton McC. Gatch, *Death: Meaning and Mortality in Christian Thought and Contemporary Culture* (New York: The Seabury Press, 1969), p. 2.
5. Jessica Mitford, *The American Way of Death* (New York: Simon & Schuster, 1963); Geoffrey Gorer, *Death, Grief, and Mourning* (Garden City, New York: Doubleday, 1965), p. xiii.
6. Gatch, *Death*, p. 171.
7. *Ibid*, pp. 172–76.
8. *Ibid.*, pp. 178, 180–81.
9. *Ibid.*, p. 181.
10. James G. Emerson, Jr., "Crisis in Adult Life," pp. 14–16; J. Paul Brown, *Counseling with Senior Citizens* (Englewood Cliffs, N. J.: Prentice-Hall, 1964); Clarence Butler, "Pastoral Needs of Older Persons: A Clinical Approach," *Journal of Pastoral Care*, vol. 22 (June, 1968), pp. 75–81; J. E. Runions, "Pastoral Care of the Elderly," *Pastoral Psychology*, vol. 23 (March, 1972), pp. 39–44; John L. Florell, ed., *Pastoral Care and Counseling Abstracts* (Richmond: National Clearing House, Joint Council on Research, 1972).
11. Allen Zacher, "Goal Rigidity as a Variable in Mid-Life and Old Age Depression," manuscript, American Association of Pastoral Counselors.
12. J. William Worden, "On Researching Death," *Pastoral Psychology*; vol. 23 (June, 1972), pp. 5–8.
13. *Ibid.*, pp. 6–7.
14. Robert J. Havighurst, *Human Development*, pp. 277–83.
15. Robert E. Neale, "Explorations in Death Education," *Pastoral Psychology*, vol. 22 (November, 1971), pp. 33–74.